Is There A
BOOK INSIDE YOU?

How to Successfully Author a Book
Alone or Through Collaboration

By Dan Poynter and Mindy Bingham

Edited by Sandy Stryker

First Edition

 Para Publishing, Santa Barbara, California

IS THERE A BOOK INSIDE YOU

How to Successfully Author a Book
Alone or Through Collaboration

By Dan Poynter and Mindy Bingham

Published by:

 Para Publishing
Post Office Box 4232
Santa Barbara, CA 93140-4232, U.S.A.

Copyright © 1985 by Daniel F. Poynter & Melinda W. Bingham
    First Printing 1985
    Printed in the United States of America

Library of Congress Cataloging-in Publication Data
Poynter, Daniel F. and Bingham, Melinda W.
    IS THERE A BOOK INSIDE YOU?
    How to Successfully Author a Book
    Alone or Through Collaboration
    Bibliography: p.
    Includes index.
    1. Authorship. 2. Authorship—Collaboration.
    I. Bingham, Mindy, 1950—. II. Title
    PN147.P66 1985   808'.02   85-12067
    ISBN 0-915516-42-X Softcover

To Wendy and Cricket for your patience

ABOUT THE AUTHORS

Mindy Bingham is the co-author of three best-selling books. *Choices, a Young Woman's Journal for Self-awareness and Personal Planning*, published in 1983, sold 80,000 copies in its first two years. *Challenges*, the boys' version, was released in 1984. A teacher's guide, British rights and a lot of well-placed book reviews soon followed. Mindy had teamed-up with a researcher/developer and a professional writer to produce these phenomenally successful books. As the eleven-year-director of the Girls Club of Santa Barbara, publishing began as a mission, turned into a fund raiser and became a going business. At the end of two years, these products have netted the Girls Club over a quarter of a million dollars.

Dan Poynter fell into publishing. He spent eight years researching a labor of love. Realizing no publisher would be interested in a technical treatise on the parachute, he went directly to a printer and "self-published." The book sold, the orders poured in and he suddenly found he was a publisher himself. Since 1969, he has written and published nineteen books on subjects from parachuting and hang gliding to computers and publishing. In the publishing field, he is widely known for his bestselling *The Self-Publishing Manual, How to Write, Print & Sell Your Own Book.*

Mindy and Dan were prompted to write this book because so many of their friends, noting their success, approached them for the secret. Now they are revealing to you the inside story on how to write a book, alone or with help,—the good life of being a published author.

CONTENTS

FOREWORD

So you are finally getting serious! You have probably had your idea for a book for some time now. Maybe you talked about it with family and friends, given it a title, even mentally out-lined a few chapters. If you are like most frustrated authors, you may not have believed that you could actually transform your ideas onto paper and profit. But now you have found this book, and you are ready to investigate how to make that transformation.

Make yourself comfortable: settle into a large, soft arm-chair, get your favorite pen and a notepad and prepare to enter the fascinating, frustrating, exhilarating and rewarding world of authorship. You are about to learn more than you could ever imagine, from two well-known authorities in the field of authoring and publishing books.

You will find this book has four sections. The first five chapters are intended to help you evaluate yourself and your topic. Take the time to read each chapter carefully and work through each exercise. Time invested in the beginning will pay off later.

The next three sections cover the mechanics of authoring a book, book collaboration and your publishing options. The processes through which Dan and Mindy guide you, build the foundation on which you can then construct the actual project itself: a tangible, readable, saleable book.

"He has half the deed done who has made a beginning." - Horace

But most of all, enjoy yourself with this book. Through it, you have two expert guides to help you explore the intriguing world of authorship. You will easily be able to decide, after completing *Is There A Book Inside You?*, how (or even whether) you want to approach your goal of authorship.

I envy the journey you are about to undertake because there are few satisfactions in life greater than holding a shiny, new book in your hands and being able to say, "I wrote this book!"

Best of luck!

Pam Deuel
Santa Barbara
July 1985

"Today's preparation determines tomorrow's achievement."

ACKNOWLEDGMENT

We have not attempted to cite in the text all the authorities and sources consulted in the preparation of this book. To do so would require more space than is available. The list would include departments of the Federal Government, libraries, industrial institutions and many individuals.

Information was contributed by Gordon Burgett, Alan Gadney, Peggy Glenn, John Kremer, John McHugh, Deborah Michelle Sanders and Jan Venolia.

We would like to give special thanks to the following people who collaborated with us on this book on collaboration:

Contributors

 Jim Comiskey, permission to adapt his self-evaluation exercises

 Heather Johnston Nicholson, manuscript ideas and direction

 Michele Jackman, business management exercises

Peer reviewers

 Charles Kent, Esquire, recommendations, approval of contracts and legal advice

 Tod Snodgrass, office supplies and machines

 Pam Deuel, overall concepts and content

Editors

 Sandy Stryker, content editing

 Barbara Greene, copy editing

Design

 Robert Howard, cover

 Carolyn Porter, book design, typesetting and pasteup

We sincerely thank all these fine people and we know they are proud of their contribution to this work.

DISCLAIMER

This book is designed to provide information in regard to the subject matter covered. It is sold with the understanding that the publisher and authors are not engaged in rendering legal, accounting or other professional services. If legal or other expert assistance is required, the services of a competent professional should be sought.

It is not the purpose of this manual to reprint all the information that is otherwise available to authors and/or publishers but to complement, amplify and supplement other texts. For more information, see the many references in the Appendix.

Book writing is not a get-rich-quick scheme. Anyone who decides to write a book must expect to invest a lot of time and effort without any guarantee of success.

Every effort has been made to make this manual as complete and as accurate as possible. However, there may be mistakes both typographical and in content. Therefore, this text should be used only as a general guide and not as the ultimate source of writing/publishing information. Furthermore, this manual contains information on writing/publishing only up to the printing date.

The purpose of this manual is to educate and entertain. The authors and Para Publishing shall have neither liability nor responsibility to any person or entity with respect to any loss or damage caused or alleged to be caused directly or indirectly by the information contained in this book.

If you do not agree with the above, you may return this book to the publisher for a full refund.

"Books are embalmed minds." - C.N. Bovee

1

WHY YOU SHOULD WRITE A BOOK

Chances are, you already know **why** you should write a book. Maybe the inspiration for your project struck all at once while you were driving the car, taking a shower, feeding the baby, or digging in the garden. Or perhaps your idea developed over a period of time, as a series of incidents convinced you that a particular book needed to be written.

For Mindy Bingham inspiration came as she stood at the front desk of the Girls Club of Santa Barbara. Mindy was touched when a single parent, struggling financially, exhausted and disillusioned, arrived to pick up her daughter. Living in poverty and feeling that she had no control over her own life, the woman had tears in her eyes as she asked Mindy, "Why didn't someone tell me what it would be like when I was growing up?"

As Mindy turned from the desk, she vowed to do something to help young women take charge of their lives—not just the teenagers in her care but as many young women as she could reach. And she knew the best vehicle for accomplishing her goal would be a book.

"A book is the only immortality." - Rufus Choats.

Dan Poynter's first book idea developed while he was managing a parachute loft in 1962. There were technical voids in parachute design and many misconceptions about parachute function. Dan was having a hard time getting his questions answered, so he set out to learn all he could about parachutes and parachuting. He began recording what he learned in a monthly column in Parachutist *magazine.*

A year and a half later, Dan realized that he was becoming an expert in the field, and that one way to help the skydivers and parachute designers was to put the answers they had been seeking in a book. The information he gathered eventually became a 592 page treatise with 2,500 illustrations.

You should write a book because there is something you need to say, or you feel there is something other people need to know. Books are the carriers of ideas and information. They are the key to personal growth and increased satisfaction. Books unlock the mind. When you write a book, you become a part of the elite community which creates our culture and keeps it alive.

The chapters which follow will tell you how to author your book and get it into print, even if you do not have the time, temperament, talent or training to be a "writer" in the traditional sense of the word.

As in many other parts of our lives today, tradition is playing a smaller role in the book business. In the past, books were luxuries available to only a few. Now they are necessities, bought and read by the millions of people who realize the importance of knowledge in a technological world such as ours. As John Naisbitt said in *Megatrends*, the new wealth is know-how.

We are experiencing an information explosion. In 1950, 17 percent of Americans were employed in information-related jobs. Today that figure has grown to more than 65 percent!

"The new source of power is not money in the hands of a few but information in the hands of many." - John Naisbitt in Megatrends

For anyone interested in authoring a book, these facts point the way to many new opportunities. Packaged information is becoming increasingly specialized. More and more books are being printed in smaller quantities. The information in them is going out of date faster, but books are being produced more rapidly by computerized equipment.

Today's customer wants condensed information—fast. People want to know "how-to" and "where-to" and they will pay well to find out. This hunger for the written word extends to works of fiction as well. Perhaps because they do not have the time to actually get away, readers reach for a book when they want escape, adventure or romance.

IS IT WORTH THE EFFORT? While writing a book is not terribly difficult, it takes time and commitment. You have only 24 hours in each day. Time can be enjoyed, employed, invested, or just dribbled away. Often it is simply lost—forever.

By investing some of that time in writing a book, you create opportunities that could change your whole life. Authoring a book may be the least expensive way of going into business for yourself. It can give you economic freedom.

During the writing process, producing a book may seem like anything *but* freedom. However, it is a trade-off. You work for the book now. It will work for you later.

Your published book can generate income for years while you are away doing something else. Someday, while you are lying on a beach or flying off to London, it will cross your mind that, "I'm getting paid for this!" You will no longer wonder if it was worth the effort.

Financial rewards are great, but there are other payoffs for writing a successful book. Some of them are:

- The fulfillment of a dream
- The pride of ownership, the satisfaction of knowing it is yours

> *"Just the knowledge that a good book is waiting one at the end of a long day makes that day happier."* - Kathleen Norris.

- The strong sense of accomplishment when you finish
- Reaching hundreds or thousands of people with your ideas
- Changing people's lives, or even the directions of institutions
- The good feeling you get whenever you get a letter from a satisfied reader
- The recognition of your peers

Most authors love the process and the outcome. They also love the pats on the head. If you were to ask them, we think they would agree that, yes, you should write a book.

"Writing a book is an adventure. To begin with, it is a toy and an amusement. Then it becomes a mistress, then it becomes a master, then it becomes a tyrant. The last phase is that just as you are about to be reconciled to your servitude, you kill the monster, and fling him to the public." - Winston Churchill

2

CAN YOU AUTHOR A BOOK?

Yes, you *can* author a book. Your knowledge and experiences are unlike those of anyone else in the world. No one looks at things in quite the way you do. Why not pass on this unique information by putting it in writing? If you have technical knowledge, a special skill, or just an interesting way of saying something, there are people waiting to buy your book.

Some people are natural writers, some are authors, and some are both. The writer is the person who puts the words on paper, while the author is the idea person. An author without interest or ability in writing can still produce a manuscript by teaming up with those who can provide the needed services—writing, researching, editing, typing, and so on.

Not that it will be easy. Authoring a book may be the most challenging project you have ever taken on. But it offers rewards unlike those you will get in any other endeavor.

The first rule of writing is to keep things manageable and in perspective. Most people have to work for a living and, therefore, can spend only a short period of time each day on their book. Trying to keep the whole project in mind, they become confused and feel overwhelmed. Often, they simply give up, feeling they will never be able to complete their manuscript. There are several tricks to overcoming this hazard. Break a mammoth project down into bite-sized chunks. Never start at page one where the hill looks steepest. Find a work-method that is compatible with your temperament, time, talent and training. Then concentrate on one section at a time and do a complete job on each one.

WHO AM I TO WRITE A BOOK? This question requires some self-reflection. You are qualified if you fall into one of these categories.

- **The Expert** is someone who has years of experience in a specific field. Experts are usually teachers, technicians or researchers. By teaching, we mean lecturing, training, writing, consulting and spreading the word. The expert has developed forms, hand-out materials and unique ways to describe the peculiarities of the field. The technician has spent time performing the occupation or activity in a hands-on fashion and can relate to the needs of the person who wants to get started in the field. The researcher usually has some recent information to share.

    Authoring a book may come easiest to experts because their subject is already well-known to them. They have a ready market because those new to a field are eager to learn what they have to say. The expert's main problem is likely to be finding enough time for writing. They tend to be extremely busy people.

    But there are reasons to try to find the time. Writing a book in your field is a learning experience. It will make you better at what you do by forcing you to reorganize, reduce, condense and clarify what you know.

Michele Jackman and Cheri Jasinski own their own management consulting firm. Their entertaining and informative lectures and workshops are well-known and highly regarded. Because of the demand for their expertise, they lead fast-paced, sometimes exhausting lives. By committing one of their favorite workshops to paper, Michele and Cheri will be able to serve more people and slow their work pace.

They completed the first draft of their book, Super Unleaded: The Accountability Process for High Performance

> " *Some people dream of worthy accomplishments, while others stay awake and do them.* "

People *by videotaping their day-long workshop, hiring a typist to transcribe the tape and then editing the hard copy for flow and understanding.*

- **The Innovator** takes a well-known, published subject and adds a new dimension to it. Innovators are often experts who notice areas in their field that need improvement, clarification, or a new approach.

In the late seventies Mindy Bingham started looking for material to use with the adolescent girls at her girls club to help them understand their career options and opportunities. When she tried to use the existing adult material with the teenagers, she discovered a "reality gap." They could not even understand why they needed to know about careers. They based their current life decisions on the notion that someone (a husband or the welfare system) was going to take care of them when they grew up. Mindy decided that a book was needed to dispel this myth and awaken young women to their future responsibilities. Choices, A Teen Woman's Journal for Self-awareness and Personal Planning, *a self-published work, sold over 40,000 copies its first year because there was nothing else like it.*

- **The Pathfinder** discovers and is fascinated by a new subject. When he or she finds there is little information available on the subject, this type of person will do the research and be the first to write a book on it. The pathfinder may not be an expert on the subject—yet. Through research, experimenting, interviewing, buying information, the pathfinder becomes the expert.

> *"I never cease to be amazed at the huge number of folks who have valuable information between their ears who don't consider packaging and selling it."* - Russ von Hoelscher.

In 1973, Dan Poynter discovered the re-emerging sport of hang gliding. He was a novice like everyone else in the sport. There were no instructors; everyone built their own gliders and taught themselves to fly. Being book-minded, he set off for the library and bookstore to see what information he could find. Unable to find a book on the subject, he wrote one. Hang Gliding, the Basic Handbook of Skysurfing *has been through the press ten times with 130,000 copies now in print. There was no competition for the book for a year and a half. Because of the recognition the book brought him, he went on to be elected to the board of the U.S. Hang Gliding Association and later President of the CIVL, The International Hang Gliding Commission. He has received a number of international awards for his organizational work in the sport.*

You may discover a new subject, something which is terribly exciting to you. Certainly you are not yet an expert in it and cannot represent yourself as one. What you do have is the inquisitiveness of a newcomer—something the veterans often lose. As you study more and more about your topic and find your answers, write them down. Soon you will become the scholar on that subject, and, with your notes, you will be one of the few people who will be able to tell the neophyte what he or she needs to know. You know what information the reader wants. And your research makes you a better practitioner.

Andy Andrews explains why he is an expert, in *How to Avoid Bicycle Theft*, as follows:

When Andy Andrews became a victim of bicycle theft himself he found he was totally unprepared. To his frustration, he discovered there was no single central source of help to advise consumers in this area. Setting himself the goal of correcting the problem Andrews spent the next several years studying

---

"We are drowning in information but starved for knowledge." - John Naisbitt in *Megatrends*.

and testing practical applications of certain procedures. He was able to come up with clear, easily followed directions to deal with the problem from both angles: first, the prevention of theft, and second, what to do if the bike is stolen. Andrews' first guide, published in 1982, proved so successful it was soon recognized as the most complete, comprehensive, and authoritative guide available to bicycle users.

One of the surest ways of producing a successful book is to be a pathfinder. The secret is to find a subject that has great potential, a large audience and has yet to be adequately covered.

- **The Artist or Creative Spirit** is a category which includes most poets and fiction writers. These story-telling artists enjoy sharing their creative thoughts, vivid imaginations, inner-most feelings and personal experiences. The novel or poem entertains or evokes emotion. Like a sculptor, painter or musician, the creative writer is an artist.

  Good fiction and poetry require a creative mind. According to Johnson O'Connor in *The Unique Individual*, only one person in four has what it takes. O'Connor says a creative writer would rate very high in the following traits:

- Creative Imagination.

- Inductive reasoning. The ability to see what seemingly diverse elements have in common.

- Analytical reasoning. Being able to organize and arrange materials logically.

- Abstract visualization. Being able to see in your mind people, places and objects that do not exist, or at least are not present to you.

- Ability to write well. Having a sizeable vocabulary and good composition skills.

"The man is most original who can adapt from the greatest number of sources." -Thomas Carlyle.

DO I HAVE WHAT IT TAKES TO WRITE A BOOK? There are no rules about who can or cannot be an author. If you evaluate your strengths and weaknesses, your assets and your limitations, you will arrive at a realistic plan that makes it possible to write a successful book. To evaluate whether you have what it takes, consider the following and then use the book author self-evaluation on the next page to make a judgment.

- Objectively evaluate the topic and unique message you wish to convey.

- Evaluate your organizational skills. Are you able to develop a well-structured outline for your book?

- Can you be dedicated to accuracy and detail? Are you prepared to devote the necessary time to researching your subject and to condensing it and transforming it in a way that will be meaningful to your readers?

- Are you committed to completing your book? Are you a starter/idea person or a starter/finisher?–Do you have discipline?

- Do you enjoy writing? Do you have the skills to write well?

- Are you able to accurately describe the pictures in your mind?

- What are your time constraints?

THE BOOK AUTHOR SELF-EVALUATION

The following quiz will help you decide if you will be able to author a book. Select the answer which best describes your feelings or talents by checking the appropriate box.

Knowledge of a Particular Topic

☐ **1.** I know the topic well and I enjoy discussing and studying it.

☐ **2.** I am reasonably confident I can learn the information needed for this topic and it appears that I will enjoy it.

☐ **3.** I am not familiar with this topic, nor do I know whether I will enjoy studying it.

Work Habits

☐ **1.** I always plan before I start a major project and then work my plan; people say I am well-organized.

☐ **2.** I find that I am organized most of the time; but on occasion, I do become distracted from my project.

☐ **3.** I take things as they come, and sometimes get priorities confused.

Accuracy and Detail

☐ **1.** I take the time to thoroughly research my work before I begin a project so I know I am doing it right.

☐ **2.** Most of the time I have all my facts correct with very few loose ends.

☐ **3.** If I can't find a fact I am looking for, I tend to feel that it is not important anyway.

Commitment

☐ **1.** I have tremendous drive and commitment, and will not stop until the project is done.

☐ **2.** I seem to have a higher level of perseverance when things are going well.

☐ **3.** I start many projects, but rarely find time to finish them.

Writing

☐ **1.** I enjoy writing and feel it comes easily to me.

☐ **2.** I enjoy writing but have to work hard at it.

☐ **3.** Although I write when I have to, it is not something I choose to do.

Writing Experience

☐ **1.** I already write professionally and feel confident in my writing talents.

☐ **2.** I dabble in writing and would like to do more.

☐ **3.** Writing sounds great and I'd like to write a book but I know I have a lot to learn about the mechanics.

Ability to Start from Scratch

☐ **1.** I enjoy the challenge of building something from scratch on my own; I'm a self-starter.

☐ **2.** If given basic guidelines, I can do a good job.

☐ **3.** I really prefer to have the entire job laid out; then I will do it well.

Time

☐ **1.** I control how I spend my time and have flexibility to work on whatever project I like.

☐ **2.** Although I have commitments that take a lot of my time, I am organized enough to find time for the things I want to do.

☐ **3.** I always feel stretched too thin and that my time is not my own.

Health

☐ **1.** I have excellent health and feel good, both physically and mentally.

☐ **2.** I get sick on occasion, but it does not last long.

☐ **3.** I have problems with my health; illness always seems to get in my way.

Self-confidence

☐ **1.** I am very confident and know that I can handle any situation.

☐ **2.** I am confident most of the time, particularly when I know the ground rules.

☐ **3.** I am not in control of my destiny; other people really control my future.

Creativity

☐ **1.** I enjoy finding solutions to problems and feel confident that, if I think about a problem long enough, the answer will come to me. I like to look at the world from many different angles.

☐ **2.** Most of the time I feel I can come up with the right answer or approach.

☐ **3.** I try really hard to come up with the right solution but sometimes it is just impossible.

Willingness to Risk Rejection

☐ **1.** I am eager to try new things and expect that if I do not fail once in a while, I am being too cautious.

☐ **2.** I want to succeed, but if I fail, I will accept it.

☐ **3.** I want to avoid failure or rejection, and will not take a risk if the project does not look like a sure thing.

Now total your score. Just add up all the checked numbers (a number one has a weight of one, a number two scores a two and a three equals three). If your total score is between 12 and 17 you are a good candidate for book authoring. If you score between 18 and 23 you may want to acquire some new skills or re-evaluate your attitude and/or aptitude. A score of 24 or more means that you should rethink your motivation and your project.

Be honest. This short personal appraisal will help you focus on your personal attributes, and it may help you decide on taking the next major step in writing your book.

DON'T MOST AUTHORS HAVE A DEGREE IN ENGLISH OR JOURNALISM? No. Those authors who do not write well get help from editors, ghostwriters or co-authors. In fact, practically every celebrity book is ghosted and most books are the effort of several people.

> *Dan Poynter, author of nineteen books and over 400 magazine articles, took only the two required English courses in college.*

> *Mindy Bingham, who graduated with a degree in animal science, took only one of the required English courses in college. She petitioned and was excused from further courses in composition.*

WHAT IF I DON'T HAVE THE TIME OR SKILL TO WRITE FINISHED COPY? No problem, this book will show you how to locate and hire co-authors, editors, ghostwriters, and other collaborators. And it will introduce you to some of the machinery available that saves time and makes writing easier.

YOUR AUTHOR WORK PLAN. On the following page you will find a self-evaluation tool to score yourself in the *Four T's of Authoring*: Temperament, Time, Talent and Training. This evaluation should help you see if you need assistance with your project and, if so, in what areas. Use this exercise, along with those on the previous pages, to judge whether or not you want to proceed with your project.

You will want to return to this guide later, when you begin to finalize your plan.

GUIDELINES FOR AN AUTHOR WORK PLAN

Circle **yes** if the statements in column one apply to you. If they do not, circle **no**.

COLUMN I	COLUMN II	
TEMPERAMENT		
I am detail oriented	yes	no
I am inquisitive	yes	no
I am well-organized and work from a plan	yes	no
I finish what I start	yes	no
TIME		
I can spend at least a couple of hours per day on my manuscript	yes	no
I can make more money writing than I can at my current job	yes	no
TALENT		
I know my topic well	yes	no
I consider myself a creative person	yes	no
I enjoy writing	yes	no
TRAINING		
I am a very good writer	yes	no
My grammar is perfect	yes	no
I enjoy writing at the typewriter	yes	no

If you circled **Yes** in Column II refer to Column III. If you circled **no** then the suggestions in Column IV may be helpful to you.

COLUMN III	COLUMN IV
If YES:	**If NO, then consider:**
Do your own research & writing	Hire a research assistant and/or editor
Do your own research & writing	Work with co-authors
Do your own research & writing	Hire an editor or writing coach
Do your own research & writing	Work with collaborators
Do your own research & writing	Work with collaborators, writing partners and/or editors
Do your own research & writing	Hire collaborators, writing partners and/or editors
Do your own research & writing	Hire research assistants or find expert co-author
Do your own research & writing	Find creative writing partner
Do your own research & writing	Collaborate with a writer
Do your own research & writing	Hire a professional writer
Do your own research & writing	Hire a professional editor
Do your own research & writing	Dictate your book and have someone else type it

O.K. SO I GET THE BOOK WRITTEN. WHAT ARE MY CHANCES OF GETTING IT PUBLISHED? Anxiety over being accepted is common among neophytes in any field. After laboring over a manuscript for hundreds or thousands of hours, you are almost certainly going to worry about whether or not it will ever be in print. Try not to let your anxiety affect your project.

It is true that few of the large book publishers will accept unsolicited manuscripts. They buy from established writers and look at manuscripts submitted (and therefore screened) by agents.

But if you are an expert in your field or have something new to say about a topic that is currently 'hot,' publishers may indeed want to see your manuscript. While trade books may be difficult to place, there are publishers who specialize in certain fields (religious books, medical books, art books, law books, etc.), and if your book falls into one of these categories, you may want to contact them. Textbook publishers are always looking for good teachers or knowledgeable professionals to write for them. Publishers of romance novels need many new titles each month and are eager to look at the manuscripts which are often sent in by their dedicated readers.

And your chances of getting your book published could be 100 percent if you make the step from author to author/ publisher. Both of the authors of this book are also self-publishers.

This book shows you how to approach publishers and also explains the very rewarding route of publishing yourself. Chapters Sixteen and Seventeen will help you select the best avenue for you and your manuscript.

YOU CAN DO IT. If all book authoring were left to the professional writers, much valuable information and many cre-

---

"In the future, editors won't tell us what to read: We will tell editors what we choose to read." - John Naisbitt in *Megatrends*

ative ideas would never make it into print. If you consider yourself an expert, innovator, pathfinder or artist, then you can author a book. If you are willing to put your energy into organization, research, recording factual information and the required follow-through, you are a prime candidate to be a published author.

In this book, we will show you several ways to bring out that book inside you. Only one has to be right for you. If one possibility "clicks," you are on your way.

In the following chapters, we will show you how to organize and write the material yourself. Then you will learn how to obtain some or all of the material and editorial help you need through collaboration with others. Finally, we will examine your publishing options to give you a better view of the entire book production process. By the time you finish this book, you will have a better understanding of how to get that 'book inside you' out—a book to share with family, friends and, possibly, the world.

"*Successful people are just ordinary people with an extraordinary amount of persistence and determination.*"

"Nothing can take the place of persistence. Talent will not; nothing is more common than unsuccessful people with talent. Genuis will not; unrewarded genius is almost a proverb. Education will not; the world is full of educated derelicts. Persistence and determination alone are ˙ the omnipotent." - Calivin Coolidge

3

WHY DO YOU WANT TO WRITE A BOOK?

WHAT DO YOU WANT FROM YOUR BOOK? Evaluating your motives will help you decide on your topic, your approach, and even if you should carry on with your project. Authors have many different reasons for spending the countless hours necessary to produce a book-length manuscript. They may seek fame, fortune, or self-actualization. They might want to help others, or record some kind of history or knowledge. You should be clear about your motives for writing a book before you begin.

- **Fame** in the traditional sense of the word conjures up thoughts of gala author parties, television talk show appearances, and whirl-wind author tours. But fame can also mean being recognized in your community or in your profession. The most satisfying type of fame for many people is when they are recognized by their peers as being successful in their field.

    It takes lots of energy to maintain the high profile that goes along with fame. As an author of a recognized work, you will be asked to speak to numerous groups, to spend time away from your family, and to give up part of your personal life. Some authors love the attention while others begin to resent the extra demands on their time and energy.

• **Fortune.** According to *The Columbia University Study of American Authors* (1981) only 5 percent of the 2,239 writers surveyed earned over $80,000 and only 10 percent over $45,000. Of those authors surveyed who wrote for a living, only 28 percent earned $20,000 or more each year. Do not let these figures discourage you; just be realistic in your approach to authoring and about the word 'fortune'.

Writing a book is an investment. After it is published, it will earn money while you are off doing something else. But how much money is it likely to earn? And how much time are you going to have to spend on it before it earns anything at all? It is important to consider these points carefully if you are writing for fortune.

Maybe you define fortune as "just earning a liveable income" from your writing. You may be writing in hopes of getting away from that nine-to-five job, in anticipation of a whole new life style. Most authors have other sources of income, at least to begin with. 46 percent of the writers surveyed in the Columbia study had full-time jobs in another field.

Many successful authors only write in their spare time. For them writing is recreation as well as a source of income. Writing provides a creative outlet while it supplements the family income.

One way to make more money on your investment is to turn your book into a business by publishing yourself. Self-publishing requires a greater commitment of time and money but may earn you up to four times as much as the common royalty would. See Chapter Seventeen on self-publishing.

• **Self-actualization** is when you need to write the book because you have a mission to accomplish. Perhaps you have a strong feeling about a subject and want to make a

---

"Writing is the only profession where no one considers you ridiculous if you earn no money." - Jules Renard

statement. Or perhaps you dream of seeing your name on the cover of a book. Friends may have said just once too often, "You should write a book about that." Maybe you want to record your family history or leave something of yourself behind in the world. Producing a book could be the fulfillment of a life-long dream.

> *Evelyn Haertig spent five years on a full-color definitive treatise entitled* Antique Combs & Purses. *A retired high school teacher and antiques dealer, she discovered there were no authoritative works on the subject. She and her photographer husband examined collections around the world. Now, she and her book are the authorities on the subject. Though this scholarly book has sold better than she projected (2,000 copies in the first year and a half), she did not expect it to make a lot of money. This book was her legacy. It was something she had to do.*

- **Helping others**   Do you want to make life better for other people? Do you have a message or a methodology you think needs to be heard? Most authors of these kinds of books work in the helping or service professions.

    A therapist or psychologist might see only 25 patients a week. With a self-help book they can reach thousands of people. Someone with a unique method of teaching first graders to read influences only 20 to 30 children at a time. By writing a book a teacher can train hundreds of instructors, thereby helping thousands of children per year.

    Your goal might be to encourage social change. A book can take a revolutionary thought, clarify it and package it. With a book, a person interested in social change can influence the course of lives, institutions, or entire societies. Many important social movements began with the publication of a book.

"What one has to do usually can be done. "- Eleanor Roosevelt

Uncle Tom's Cabin by Harriet Beecher Stowe brought attention to slavery and fueled the abolition movement. The Feminine Mystique, *written in 1964 by Betty Friedan, is considered the force that initiated the women's movement.* Rachel Carson's Silent Spring *sparked the environmental movement. Ralph Nader's 1965 book* Not Safe at Any Speed *dealt the deathblow to the Corvair.* Black Beauty *by Anna Sewell fostered the movement against cruelty to animals.* The Complete Book of Running, *a 1977 book by Jim Fixx, helped to generate interest in the fitness revolution. Charles Dickens used books to bring attention to the plight of the lower class of Great Britain. Each of these people saw something new, important and shocking. Their writing, whether fiction or nonfiction, changed the thinking of society.*

- **Recording history, knowledge or expertise** Until recently, books were the only way we had to pass on our knowledge, our history, and our culture. Despite other forms of media, books are still one of the best, most efficient, and most economical ways to inform people of our shared past, our discoveries, and our lives.

    The Library of Congress holds over eighty-million volumes, each adding something to our collective pool of knowledge. Perhaps you, too, have valuable information or observations to pass on.

OTHER REASONS for writing a book might include:

- **Spending your spare time constructively** For people who love words, writing can be an especially nice hobby. Whether you like to write poems, stories, novels, memoirs, or whatever, writing can be relaxing, enlightening, and, in many ways, rewarding.

- **Career advancement** For many professionals and academics, publishing books and articles is a 'must,' in order to gain tenure, get promoted, or be noticed.

> *"The most powerful factors in the world are clear ideas in the minds of energetic men (and women) of good will."* - J. Arthur Thomson

- **Teaching tools** Some very successful books came about because their authors needed a manual or a book for their own students or clients, or to explain their inventions. Are you frustrated by a lack of the precise book you need in your work? Write it!

> *Barbara Harris was unable to find a suitable cookbook for her class in microwave cooking, so she wrote and published her own for the use of her students. Soon others heard about Barbara's cookbook and began calling to request copies. She expanded her marketing, and, ten years later, more than 500,000 copies of her classic* Let's Cook Microwave *are in print.*

WHAT I WANT FROM MY BOOK

Indicate your most important reasons for writing a book. Place a "1" next to your prime motive, a "2" beside the next most important reason and so on (if you have more than two reasons).

_____ Fame

_____ Fortune

_____ Self-actualization

_____ Helping others

_____ Recording history and knowledge

_____ Other: (Describe) _____

"It wouldn't matter if I never sold a book because my book has made my seminars and consulting possible" - Jim Comiskey.

YOUR MOTIVES FOR WRITING WILL AFFECT WHAT YOU WRITE If you chose either fame or fortune as a top priority, you will have to write for a large market. The topic will have to be useful to hundreds of thousands of people. A well-written, exciting novel is one way to meet these objectives. To achieve fame with a non-fiction book, you need to excel in a field that is currently popular: psychology, relationship advice, health, sex, diet, or finance are a few.

If you want the fortune and wish to avoid fame, write under a pen name. In 1970, "J" wrote *The Sensuous Woman*, a best-seller. Perhaps because the subject was controversial at the time, the author was not revealed. But you can bet the royalty checks found their way to the author.

> *Mary P., who has a top scientific position with a major corporation, writes romance novels on the side. She feels she might be less effective with her all-male staff if they knew about her hobby, so she publishes under a pen name. Still, her writing enables her to pursue her other love—sports cars. Her royalty checks were used for a brand new Porsche.*

If your priorities are self-actualization, helping others, or recording history, an unusually large market may not be as important to you as it might be if your prime motives are fame and/or fortune. But your work must still have a reasonably large potential audience. Publishers are in business to make money. Your motivation for authoring a book must be kept in mind when choosing your topic, but you must also consider your options for attracting a publisher if that is the route you want to take.

WHAT DO YOU WANT FROM YOUR FICTION OR POETRY? A priority for many fiction writers is fame and/or fortune. The fame and the fortune can grow to tremendous

> *"I'm not trying to be taken seriously by the East Coast literary establishment. But I'm taken very seriously by the bankers."* - Judith Krantz.

proportions if you become a "great American novelist." In recent years advances of over $1 million have been paid to established writers like Norman Mailer, John Irving, Arthur C. Clark, Rosemary Rogers, Barbara Taylor Bradford, and Danielle Steele. Judith Krantz's *Princess Daisy* brought in $3.2 million in paperback reprint fees alone. These kinds of figures are what keep thousands of hopeful novelists at their typewriters working late into the evening.

Fiction can be used by the author to help others. John Ballard's Monsoon *is a good example of a book with a fictional character, MacBurnie King, who is determined to do something about world hunger. This action-packed novel entertains the teenage audience with adventure and suspense but at the same time creates an awareness of the needs of people suffering from hunger. John feels strongly about the problem of world hunger and the book is his way of contributing to its solution.*

Most poets write for self-actualization. And most poets do not make a living from poetry. But they feel they have something to share with others and so they labor on.

Although you might think that recording history would be solely the work of nonfiction writers, many novelists have produced factual novels. These writers, may take some literary liberties, but their works are helpful in understanding critical times. Herman Wouk's *The Winds of War* and *War and Remembrance* are two such books. Most events in these novels about World War II are true and the author made sure of their accuracy. And because the readers were so involved in the emotional lives of the fictional characters, many people experienced, understood and appreciated the events of the time in a much more personal way than would have been possible reading a textbook on the war.

"The reward of a thing well done, is to have done it." - Ralph Waldo Emerson

Once you have decided **why** you want to write a book, you are ready to decide **what** to write.

"*Years ago, to say you were a writer was not the highest recommednation to your landlord. Today, he at least hesitates before he refuses to rent you an apartment—for all he knows you may be rich.*" - Arthur Miller

4

WHAT KIND OF BOOK
DO YOU WANT TO WRITE?

You probably would not be reading this book if you did not have some idea of what you want to write. Before you make a final decision on your topic, take a look at some of the books being written today.

WHAT KIND OF BOOK WILL YOU WRITE? Will it be fiction (romances, children's books, westerns, mysteries) or nonfiction (how-to's, cookbooks, history, artbooks or travel)? Once you decide on the type of book you plan to write, check the resources in the *Appendix*. There you will find the titles of several books devoted to the writing and production of specific subjects with more detailed information than we could possibly include here.

FICTION may be generally categorized as mysteries, suspense novels, adventures, westerns, romances, historical novels, science fiction, juveniles or young adult, children's books, Gothics, and general novels.

> *"Fiction is an art and comes from emotion; nonfiction is a craft and comes from information."*

● **Children's books**. With twenty million youngsters under five years in the U.S., there is a large market for children's books. This market will continue to grow because of the current baby boom. Many couples are delaying the start of their families until established in their careers. Therefore they have more disposable income to spend on their children. These parents tend to be well-educated. They value books and learning and want their children to enjoy reading.

Children's books and juveniles may be categorized as follows:

Ages 3-4 through 7-8	Picture books
Ages 8 through 12:	Fiction and nonfiction
Ages 9 through 12:	Humorous novels
Ages 11 through 18:	Special interest books

Children's books can be the most difficult to write. You must be accurate (children are not as forgiving as adults) and you must have a keen understanding of the children of the current generation.

In writing for children, you have a greater responsibility because children are less able to discriminate between good and bad ideas. For example, in the 80s, authors have a responsibility in their writing to be nonsexist, nonviolent and to promote self-sufficiency—particularly for girls. Fantasies should be constructive. Think back to your own childhood. Which stories are still with you—which books shaped your life?

Illustrations can provide half the charm and interest of a picture book, so most children's book writers must be artists or must collaborate with an artist. See Chapter Twelve on collaboration and the Appendix for books on how to write for children.

> *"Children's books are written to be read; adult books are written to be talked about at cocktail parties."* - Lloyd Alexander.

- **Romance novels** may account for 30 percent of all the fiction sold in the early 1980s—in March of 1985, the one-billionth Harlequin romance came off the press. This fiction offers release and escape for millions of people. Readers like the action, sex and romance, and many identify with the characters.

   Romances are written for different audiences. Historical romances are longer stories with more adventure and historical background material, period romances concentrate on a certain historical period, and contemporary romances have a modern heroine.

   Silhouette, a well-known New York publisher, receives about 500 unsolicited manuscripts a month. And the romance publishers actually advertise for unknown authors. Because the romance novel has a formula, it may be easier for the first time author to write successfully.

   Silhouette reports that each of its titles sells between 250,000 and one million copies at two or three dollars per book. Royalties average between 6 and 8 percent of the wholesale price. A successful and prolific author for one of the large romance publishers can count on earning between $50,000 and $300,000 per year.

   If you want to investigate romance writing, see the resources in the Appendix.

- **Confessions** are fictional personal experience stories, usually meant to inspire hope in the reader. They provide examples the readers may look to for guidance and solutions to their problems.

   Confession themes are simple: it takes two to ruin a marriage; if you make a sacrifice for another, happiness will come to you; you always pay for your sins. Basically, there are three types of confessions: The shocker (drugs, sex, witchcraft), the tear-jerker (about the dead, dying or handicapped) and the conflict (romance, family).

"We romantic writers are there to make people feel and not think. A historical romance is the only kind of book where chastity really counts."
- Barbara Cartland

- **Novels** Novelists are the storytellers of the world. They must have a burning desire to write—as well as the time, ability and freedom to do it. Are you imaginative and good with words? Do you love to write? Are you disciplined and well-organized? If so, you may have the makings of a novelist.

    Fiction is entertainment and must compete for the reader's time with television, the beach and taking the kids to the zoo. A lot of fiction is written each year but comparatively little is published. You might be more successful in selling your fiction if you consider your audience first. Stories tailored to a specific geographic area might sell well locally.

IF YOU HAVE CHOSEN TO WRITE FICTION you should be aware that publishers in the United States receive more than 30,000 manuscripts annually, uninvited and unannounced. Of the 2,000 novels published in 1981 most were written by accomplished authors. Only a few were written by unknowns or first-time authors.

But, publishers are still buying first-time authors. They say the public wants fresh approaches. So it is not impossible to get your first book published. What you need are talent, tenacity, and the ability to persuade a publisher or agent to read your manuscript.

Jean Auel's first novel The Clan of the Cave Bear *brought her an advance of $130,000 from Crown Publishers and within the first two years of production, the book had earned her over $675,000.*

Once you are a known author you can command large advances. Author Erich Segal (Love Story) received $1 million for his book The Class, *released in April, 1985.*

> *"No wonder poets have to seem so much more business-like than businessmen—Their wares are so much harder to get rid of."* - Robert Frost.

Fiction writers who are ready for the test may send their manuscript to a magazine entitled the *West Coast Review of Books* for review. A good review here will get the attention of several publishers. Send for a sample copy or subscribe to the magazine to see what they do (address in the *Appendix*).

For more information on selling unpublished novels, see the January 1983 edition of *Writer's Digest*. For a list of fiction publishers, see *Fiction Writer's Market* and Alan Gadney's *How-to Enter & Win Fiction Writing Contests*, listed in the Appendix.

Creativity in nonfiction is nice. In fiction, it is critical. You are producing entertainment and must be able to tell a story well. How you say it may even be more important than what you say.

Fiction can be more difficult to place with a publisher. The competition is very keen. But the potential for great financial rewards is there. According to *The Columbia University Study of American Authors* (1981) of 2,239 writers, genre fiction (romance, mysteries, Gothics) is the most lucrative kind of writing, with 20 percent of its authors earning over $50,000 annually from their books and stories.

POETRY does not sell well except in a very few cases. Even if you can sell a poem to a magazine, the payment is likely to be $20. In fact, most of the poetry magazines pay only by sending the author some free copies of the magazine. According to *The Columbia University Study of American Authors*, 55 percent of the authors earning less than $2,500 from writing were poets or those writing academically oriented nonfiction.

Poetry, once created, must be shared and given exposure. Attend poetry readings, mail your work off to poetry magazines and talk to other poets. Once you have received feedback from your readings and magazine exposure, you may select a grouping for publication in a book. The book should be a cohesive work with a central theme so that an audience can identify with it. Write to the American Poetry Association for a free copy of *Poet's Guide to Getting Published*

"My books are water; those of great geniuses are wine—everybody drinks water." - Mark Twain.

(P.O. Box 2279-P, Santa Cruz, CA 95063). Send $4.60 for a copy of *How to Enter Poetry Contests to WIN* by Leiper to The Inkling, (P.O. Box 128-P, Alexandria, MN 56308). The *Directory of Poetry Publisher* ($10 ppd.) lists over 1,000 markets for poets (Dustbooks, P.O. Box 100-P, Paradise, CA 95969). Poets should keep in touch by subscribing to *CODA: Poets & Writers Newsletter* (201 West 54th Street, New York, NY 10019).

NONFICTION does not require any great literary style. It is simply the sale of well researched, reorganized, updated and, most important, repackaged information. Of course, it is helpful if you can write well but the content of the work is more important than the presentation of it. If you are a paint-by-the-numbers artist, you may lack the creativity for good fiction. If you opt for nonfiction and are unable to write beautifully, this book will show you how to find and work with other people who will put the zip into your material.

Nonfiction books usually have a distinct purpose which may be to inform (history, biography, exposes), to teach (how-to), to persuade (public relations), to interest and to entertain (most autobiographies, travel) and/or to inspire (arouse emotion.) What counts in nonfiction is a good idea which is fresh and sharply focused—specific information on a specific topic.

The subjects with the best sales potential are how-to's, money, health, self-improvement, hobbies, sex and psychological well-being. Find a need and fill it. There are many types of nonfiction.

- **How-to's**   Most adults turn to books when they want to find out how to do something. We are a nation of do-it-yourselfers. There are how-to books on just about anything you want to learn. Most magazine articles and one-third of the books are how-to.

> *"If you want to get rich from writing, write the sort of thing that's read by persons who move their lips when they're reading to themselves."* - Don Marquis.

Jim Capossela published articles, photographs and drawings in a number of outdoors magazines. He turned out a book on sport crabbing and then wrote on how to do it all with Write For The Outdoors Magazines. *This author, publisher and entrepreneur now operates the* Northeast Sportsman's Press.

One specialized book that has been selling for years is Kershner's The Student Pilot's Flight Manual *which has gone through the press 26 times for 485,000 copies.*

Every new national craze requires factual how-to books. And, at the rate our world is changing, opportunities for writing how-to books are everywhere. Your project could be anything from a technical manual for professionals in a given field, to an easy-to-follow text for anyone interested in your subject.

See the Appendix for titles of books you might like to consult (and notice how many books there are on how to write a book!)

- **Self-improvement** According to *Newsweek* there are over 1,300 books on fitness and health currently in print. Popular subjects like running are covered by many books. Some books are general while others treat a specific portion of the activity. Besides sports, there are books telling you how to eat, drink, dance, work, speak, buy, sell, play, find a job, divorce and even how to get married again.

- **Local books** are relatively easy to write and market. The information and the distribution are local, making them an ideal project for the beginning writer and self-publisher. Tourist guides, restaurant guides and historical books are indeed an easy way to get started. The monetary success of these publications depends on the size of the geographical area and the amount of tourism. For example, in California, a book on Los Angeles might make more money than one on Bakersfield. On the other hand, competition in L.A. is likely to be keener.

Judy Dugan had gathered information for a guide book but did not know how to proceed. She worked for a typesetter and one day found herself pasting up The Self-Publishing Manual. *Armed with the answer, she approached a new bank in town about using her book as a premium. The bank bought it and she had thirty days to finish writing her book, typeset it, paste it up, print it and deliver 5,000 copies. She made the deadline and the bank gave a copy of* Santa Barbara Highlights and History *to everyone who came in during its opening week. The bank even hosted an autograph party for her. She printed 10,000 books and was on her way, selling the rest through local museums and other tourist attractions.*

- **Directories** are relatively easy to compile and are good for people who love digging up information. Your directory might cover anything from the bed and breakfast establishments in your town to a list of reviews on a certain type of book (computers, for example).

    Mary June Kay published a bibliography of romance authors and titles to help readers find their favorite authors. Authors of romance novels often write under many different pen names.

    John Kremer mailed questionnaires to printers and print buyers and then assembled the information into his Directory of Short-run Book Printers.

    Maggie Kleinman found a subject and then found her material. The result is her Writer's Guide to Southern California *which is full of resources for writers*

    One advantage to directories is that those listed in them are often prime potential buyers. Therefore, as you compile your directory, you are building a mailing list.

- **Kits** are similar to directories. They are collections of all the forms and information necessary to start a business, promote a product or get listed in all the applicable directories.

Lawless J. Barrientos publishes his Starting Business Kits. *He provides blank forms, instructions, filled-in examples, lists of tax due dates and directories of important agencies. Since government forms vary, he has collections for every state. Originally, he put the kit together for his own clients. Once tested in the field, he began selling it to others. He started with direct mail advertising, sold it in office supply stores and wholesaled it to the Florida Chamber of Commerce.*

Dan Poynter collects forms and applications for book publishers and sells them in a folder as Publishing Forms. *With the kit, new publishers are able to get their books listed in all the applicable directories easily, submit them to all wholesalers quickly and register them with the proper agencies correctly. While his bestselling book,* The Self-Publishing Manual *tells readers where to write for the forms, many publishers still send for the kit to save time.*

- **Cookbooks** are among the most popular of nonfiction books. Everyone eats and most people cook—there is a large market for cookbooks. Working people who do not have time for extensive cooking probably need more help with quick-to-prepare meals. Of the some 40,000 books published each year, about 500 are cookbooks.

  There are four general cookbook categories: basic (general), specialty (crock pot, chocolate, etc.), status (what the "beautiful people" are cooking), and public relations (used to promote a product or enterprise, e.g. microwave ovens). The general cookbooks are the hardest to sell because the competition is so great. A small, easily targeted market is best if you have a way to reach it.

Joyce Carlisle had over an acre of avocado trees and was faced with a glutted market. In order to stimulate the sale of avocados nationwide, she wrote and published the Avocado Lovers Cookbook. *Her interest in farming and cooking lead her to writing and publishing.*

- **Life stories** are often compiled by grandparents as a gift for their children and grandchildren. *Roots* made everyone conscious of their family tree and encouraged millions of people to conduct geneological searches. But while *Roots* was a major bestseller, most life stories are self-published in small quantities for the benefit of the immediate family. This makes an excellent project for the family historian, who is sure to be immortalized as the person who took the time to preserve the family's treasured past for generations to come.

  According to Robin Hilborn, over 1,500 people are publishing newsletters in their own family names. With 2.2 million Smiths in the United States, it is understandable there are eight Smith newsletters. There are over 100,000 people in the United States with names such as Keller, Franklin, Jensen, Harvey, Weber and Ray. A book tracing your family might have quite a good market. Start by sending $5.00 for *Hilborn's Family Directory* (42 Sources Blvd #52, Pointe Claire, PQ, H9S 2H9, Canada) which lists existing newsletters and contains a lot of other fascinating genealogical information. Then write Sharon Taylor (Halbert's, Inc., Bath, OH 44210) for a price quote on the story of your family name (about $30).In addition to a lot of good genealogical background on your family name, she includes an address list of households with your name in the United States. Once you write your book, use this mailing list to sell it.

- **Autobiographies**   Unless you are famous, there usually is not a large market for your autobiography. But if you are a well-known figure or associated with a famous person or event, making a deal with one of the large publishing companies to publish your story could be lucrative. In 1984 Geraldine Ferraro was paid a reported $700-900,000 advance to write her autobiography. Jeanne Kirkpatrick, retired from her United Nations position, received a rumored $300,000 advance for her memoirs.

- **Religious** and inspirational books have always sold well and are now moving better than ever. Of course, the *Holy Bible* ranks as the number one bestseller of all time.

- **Photographic books** are usually produced by people who are photographers first and writers second. These books take many forms. They may be monographs (presenting the photographer's personal view of life), in-house books (like the *Time-Life* books), illustrated trade books (usually covering a single subject), or how-to books (photos are used to illustrate the text).

  Andy Keech has published three volumes of Skies Call. *The full-color coffee table books, packed with unusual action shots of skydiving, contain very little writing.*

  Brad Elterman published Shoot the Stars, *and tells how you can become a celebrity photographer. Sprinkled with photos of movie stars and other famous people, Brad tells how he took the shot and reveals how to break into the business.*

- **Business and professional books** are on a sharp sales increase. Business people realize it is far cheaper and faster to buy condensed, targeted information from you than to start from scratch and figure it all out for themselves. Business people can afford to invest in books and their purchases may be more impulsive since they are spending company money, not personal funds.

  Tom Peters' book, *In Search of Excellence*, sold more than four million copies. *A Passion for Excellence*, his new book (with co-author Nancy Austin), sold a quarter of a million copies in its first month in the stores.

  There may be more money publishing your information in short monographs than in longer books. Monographs are concise booklets packed with valuable information that the average person could read in an hour or two. Timely monographs usually command a higher unit price, can be published in shorter runs and take less time to produce. But monographs must be up-to-date and filled with valuable information for a well-targeted audience to command top dollar.

- **Travel books** should be tightly focused (a golfer's guide to the Northeast or the wineries of Santa Barbara County). It is not likely you can effectively compete with the large general guide books like Fodor's or Michelin.

    The best part of a travel book is the research—all that very deductible travel.

- **History books** usually tell of an interesting period or event. While they may or may not have wide appeal, they are sure to sell locally.

    Mason Philip Smith spent years researching a little known event, the Confederate raids in and around Maine during the Civil War. His search for information lead him to unpublished documents in the hands of one of the raider's descendents. He put it all in Confederates Downeast. *While many people knew of Confederate naval attacks in northern waters, few knew about the land actions via Canada.*

- **Science/Technical books** deal with such fields as medicine, science and engineering. Sales in this category have increased greatly in recent years. Most books have a limited professional audience, but there are exceptions. For example, Masters' and Johnson's *Human Sexual Response* became a bestseller.

- **Textbooks** may sell for years and years with periodic updates or revisions. Writing a text now may produce returns over a long period of time. Authors of textbooks need not be recognized experts in their field when they begin writing.

"Colors fade, temples crumble, empires fall, but wise words endure."
- Edward Thorndike

Many are just good teachers who see how the books currently available to them and their students could be improved. Of course, after writing a well-regarded book, they do become recognized as authorities in their field.

- **Anthologies** are collections of chapters from several different experts on the same subject area. To produce an anthology, outline the total book; decide what you want it to accomplish. Detail what you feel should be covered in each chapter. Then find experts in each area to write on those topics.

- **Re-publishing articles** Many author/publishers have gone the easy route by simply editing the material of others. Deeply interested in an area, they have thoroughly researched a subject only to find that many fine experts have already written good material on several aspects of it. The collection of these articles, one per chapter, form a book.

  To pursue this course, contact each author for permission to use the material and ask him or her to edit a photocopy of the piece (there may be new information, or the author may want to change something). This makes your chapter better than the original article. If the chapter must be shortened, ask the author to do it. This is faster and easier than doing it yourself and then negotiating your changes with him or her.

  If, for example, you are deeply involved in the sport of parachuting, you might contact the national association and its magazine about gathering like articles which have appeared over the years and re-publishing them in a series of booklets. Booklet Number One might consist of all the best articles on student training. Your primary market would be the members of the association: you would sell them through the organization's "store" and via mail order by advertising in the magazine. Thus, the association is providing both the material and the customers. As an editor, you simply repackage the information.

When re-publishing articles, do not offer royalties to the original authors. Payments split between so many people would be small and the accounting would be overwhelming. Buy the material outright or simply offer the authors the immortality that comes from being in a book. A small honorarium and five copies of the book will be more than enough for most people.

- **Out of print books** may be purchased and reworked. Updating older material is usually easier than starting from scratch and you should be able to tap the same market as the older work. Citing the out of print material as the major source for your book will attract some of the original buyers.

> *Bill Kaysing discovered an out-of-copyright book called* Thermal Springs of the World. *He abstracted just the data on hot springs in the western United States, added some original comments and republished the work as* Great Hot Springs of the West. *Review copies sent to several major magazines resulted in an entire column of flattering coverage in* Sunset *magazine. $3.00 orders poured in for a book that cost him fifty cents to print and some 3,000 copies were sold in a little over a year.*

Whatever your interests or abilities, the preceding list should give you some ideas. Pick a category that appeals to you and read the next chapter before selecting a subject.

"The world is before you, and you need not take it or leave it as it was when you came in." - James Baldwin

5

IS YOUR TOPIC A WINNER?

If you want to **sell** a book, not simply to write it or see it in print, you must evaluate the market size and research the competition before you make a final decision on your topic.

Once you are convinced that the subject is a good one, you are ready to choose a working title and write your back cover copy. These exercises will give you something to hang on to, something to guide your project as you get on with the meatiest part of authoring a book.

IF YOUR CHOICE IS NONFICTION, picking a subject is your first step. You may already know what it is; you may, for example, wish to record a lifetime of experience in your field of expertise. If you come up with more than one book idea, select the easiest one with the widest market.

Selecting a topic is not a weekend adventure. Your book and its subject will be with you a long time. If you produce a recognized work, you will become identified with it.

Whether or not you have settled on a subject, go through the following exercise.

"A book is a success when people who haven't read it pretend they have."

BOOK TOPIC/AUTHOR EXPERTISE EVALUATION

Book topic:_____

Author's area of expertise:_____

To help you decide whether the book topic is right for you, write **yes** or **no** in front of the following questions:

( ) Is your information on your subject up-to-date?

( ) Do you work or participate in the field, or are you recently retired from it?

( ) Do you receive **daily** feedback on your expertise from your customers, people in the field?

( ) Do you read all the literature, attend all the conferences and continue to collect information?

( ) Do you have practical expertise as well as the required theoretical knowledge?

( ) Do people in the field recognize you for your contributions?

( ) Do you have a reputation for originality and innovation?

( ) Have you received any awards or patents in your field?

( ) Do you have the organization and discipline necessary to not only produce a book, but to project the image of an authority?

( ) Are you businesslike?

If you have answered **yes** to a large percentage of the questions, you may be prepared to author a book on your topic.

CONSIDER THE ELEMENTS necessary for producing successful nonfiction:

1. **The subject is interesting to you.** If you are interested in the subject, working on it will be exciting. If you are not interested, the work will be drudgery and you are not likely to do as good a job.

2. **You have the necessary expertise and the information is available.** Remember, nonfiction depends upon past experiences or research or, best of all, both. The book should be on a subject in which you are an expert or would like to become an expert. You have spent years working at, specializing in, and learning something and there are thousands of people out there willing to pay good money to get the short course on it. Write what you know!

   If you select your hobby for a book subject, there are a number of advantages: you already know what has been written, you have the contacts for gathering more information and your further participation in that hobby will become tax deductible.

3. **The subject is of interest to others and is, therefore, saleable.** Few people will purchase your autobiography unless you are already famous. Protest subjects usually have a short life and built-in audience limitations. As entertainment, fiction must compete with other media such as television and films which require less conscious work. All can be and have been successful books, but you must know the limitations and competitiveness of these areas.

   Anticipate reader interest and pick a subject which will sell on its own even if the buyer has never heard of you.

"How vain it is to sit down to write when you have not stood up to live." - Henry David Thoreau

4. **The subject matter is tightly focused. We are in an age of specialization.** People want information on specific subjects.

5. **The market is easy to reach.** Is the potential market so well defined that by attending a few choice conventions or by receiving reviews in a few key magazines and journals the majority of the buyers will know about your book?

    If there are magazines on the subject, what are their circulations? If there are clubs, how many members do they have? If mailing lists are available, how big are they?

6. **The market for the subject is large enough to justify your investment of time and money.** How large is the market? Obviously the market for diet books is much larger than one on repairing wicker furniture. But there are thousands of people who work with wicker furniture either professionally or as a hobby and they may be easier to identify and reach with a targeted sales message.

    How many people should be interested and how many can you attract to your product?

    • Identify the buyer.

    • How many people are there in this category in the United States?

    • Will all of these people buy the book? If not, how many?

    • What is the international appeal?

    • What other markets are there besides book stores and libraries?

    For example, there are 25,000 active skydivers in the U.S. How many will buy your book on student parachutist training? Are you selling to parachuting students or parachuting instructors? How many instructors are there? Can you sell them all? Would the U.S. Parachute Association adopt your book as an instructor's resource? Could you make money selling 500 copies a year if the price were higher and the sales went on year after year?

What is the potential size of your market? Be conservative on this one. Just because you are writing a book on outboard motor overhaul does not mean that every owner of the eight million motor boats in the U.S. will buy it.

Does the topic have international appeal? Although harder to reach, what about the foreign market? But be realistic. Expanding to Canada does not double your market. The population of Canada is less than that of California and part speaks only French.

Is there more than one market? The large publishers serve the book trade: bookstores and libraries. Fiction sells best there. Nonfiction usually sells better when you can reach the users directly. Can you sell the book by mail to a well-targeted audience? Are there hobby stores that might carry it? Can you sell it to schools or organizations? If the bookstores pick it up, so much the better. But to smaller nonfiction publishers, the bookstore sales are the frosting, not the cake.

If the market for the book is not large and you justify its creation because you just have to get it out of your system, fine. But you must realize from the beginning this project will not be a great money-maker. It may be reward enough to have a book to share with friends and family.

As one woman said about her self-published book on needlepoint designs of the 18th century, "I produced this book in lieu of a trip to Europe this year. The excitement I get when I fill an order out-shines the good feelings I get over coffee at a bistro on the Avenue des Champs-Elysees."

"*The profession of book-writing makes horse racing seem like a solid, stable business.*" - John Steinbeck.

MARKET SIZE

Circle the numbers of the statements that describe the book you are thinking of writing. To be financially successful, the subject of the book should meet at least one of the following criteria:

1. It is on a subject as yet unknown but of wide potential interest.

2. It is on a subject in which you are a recognized authority.

3. It is on a subject which will have an impact on many people in many ways.

4. It is on a subject which has not yet been covered or one where you have a fresh angle.

5. It is on a subject of recent high-level interest, a subject on which people want more current information.

6. It is on a subject that empowers people to take their life and life decisions into their own hands.

7. It covers a subject that teaches people a skill they would otherwise pay a specialist many times the cover price to perform.

WHO WILL BUY MY BOOK? WHO WILL READ MY BOOK?
Before you even sit down at the keyboard to write, you must decide who is going to buy your book. Who will need it? You must direct your writing toward a particular group of people. Be realistic. First start by defining who will be the purchaser of the book. Will it be the person who will actually read the book, or a third party such as a librarian? Or will the book be a gift item from a parent to a child? Think about the obvious purchasers and maybe the not so obvious.

While you might tend to focus on a topic with the largest number of possible readers, sometimes a book on a narrow topic is better because it is unique and therefore can corner the market.

In 1985, Marilyn Grams, M.D., began writing a book about a breastfeeding technique she pioneered for working women. Her initial idea was to write a general book on breastfeeding incorporating her specialized information into the body of the book. This way, she felt, she would have a bigger audience. But she changed her strategy and redirected the book toward the working mother. She realized that there were a number of books on breastfeeding. Her book had a unique message. And statistics show that a narrowly focused book— breast feeding for working mothers—was really not such a narrow market as one would imagine. In 1984 over 45 percent of mothers with children under the age of one year worked outside the home. Even more important, the working mother will identify more closely with this book than with a generalized breastfeeding book. Dr. Grams' Breastfeeding Success for Working Mothers *is unique. Like her, find your niche in the market.*

Women provide a growing market for nonfiction books. Many women have entered the world of business. Once in the work force they are also faced with a shortage of time. They need information and their employment provides them with the money to pay for it. Books aimed at women have great sales potential.

RESEARCH YOUR COMPETITION—If you know your field, you probably already know some of your competition. To determine whether your book subject has already been adequately covered, go to the:

I. LIBRARY

   A.   Ask the reference librarian for Bowker's *Books in Print* which lists all books currently available by subject, title and author. Start with the subject volumes but also look under title and check on the people who write in this field in the author volumes. Search the *Forthcoming BIP* book for recent books. Make a list of those books you would like to review or research. Take a pocket-full of coins and photocopy these pages. Photocopying is faster and you will want to refer to these pages later at home. Interestingly, you will find later that some of the books listed in *BIP* never went to press.

   Using a red pen on your photocopies, underline the publisher (do they publish other books in this field?), the publishing date (is it an old book?), the author (is he or she well-known in the field?).

   If you find a number of similar books in your area, check the copyright dates. Old books may be out of print. Call the publishers and ask if new editions are planned. If the answer is "yes", ask how many are "in print"; the subject must be a good one. If it is "no", you will not have any competition.

   When looking up competitive titles, check the prices. If they are all high-priced hardcover editions, you may be able to compete with a lower-priced softcover edition. If you find your topic has been covered extensively and recently, you need to evaluate what makes your book unique. Are you an innovator who can bring a new dimension to the subject?

B. Check the library's catalog card file or microfiche to see which of the books you want to research may be obtained there. Other books may be purchased at your local bookstore or by writing directly to the publisher; addresses are listed in the back of *Books in Print*. And remember that this is probably not the only library in town. Try the local college too; it will have different types of books.

Rate the other books as you read them:

1. Is the author an expert?
2. Is the book well-written?
3. Is the subject well-covered? (what is left out?)
4. What is unique about the book? And how can you do better?

C. Research the *Reader's Guide to Periodical Literature* which lists magazine articles on every subject.

D. Interview an acquisitions librarian. Ask if your proposed book would fit in with the library's collection and if the librarian would order one. Do patrons of the library ask for material on your topic?

Ask the reference librarians for help in locating material. This is their job and they love it. If you mention that you may write a book on this subject, all the better. Librarians hold authors in high esteem.

II. BOOKSTORE   Next, visit a bookstore and:

A. Check the shelves to see what is available in the subject area you are exploring. Look everywhere, some bookstores catalog books in strange places.

B. Ask to view the bookstore's microfiche cards. If refused, try another bookstore. Each week, the stores receive inventory cards from Baker & Taylor, Ingram, Bookpeople and others wholesalers. The books listed on the fiche are available to the bookstores from the wholesaler. The microfiche cards and reader are usually found near *Books In Print* at the special order desk.

Is there another book like yours? Titles and books which appear to be like yours are usually different. In any case, you must obtain samples—to check on the competition and later for research.

C. Pitch your idea to the manager of the bookstore. Is your idea suitable for the book trade? Would it sell in a bookstore? Would the manager buy it? What types of books are people buying? A note of caution... survey at least 20 bookstores. One or two negative or glowing responses could cloud your opinion.

III. *PUBLISHERS WEEKLY*, the trade magazine of publishers, available at your library, will tell you what is coming next season. Check especially the display advertising and the *Forecast* section.

IV. **MARKET SURVEY**   If you still are not ready to commit your time and money to the project, try a market survey. Draft a form letter and send it to people in the field asking if they will buy the book. For example, if you had a children's cookbook, you would contact people in catalog houses and children's shops with a detailed description and ask them if there is a need and how many they would stock.

V. WRITE AN AD   Some people place an ad in periodicals to test the saleability of a new book—before they write it.

> *Melvin Powers drafts and places ads for a book similar to one he is planning. If the ad pulls well, he ships the competitive book and begins writing his own. This system tests both the subject and his ad copy.*

Once you have decided on your topic you need to focus it. What will make your work special? By writing your back-cover copy you are forced to define precisely what you mean to say in your book. This copy will help keep you on the right path while you complete your manuscript.

WRITE YOUR BACKCOVER COPY BEFORE YOU WRITE YOUR BOOK   You should be able to convey the whole idea of your book in a single sentence and describe the contents of the book in a single typewritten page.

Your back cover is important sales space. Use it for your pitch. If the spine of your book conveys a clear message through a provocative title, the potential buyer will pull it from the shelf. If the cover is interesting enough, he or she will turn the book over to see what it is about. People average about 15 seconds reading the back cover, so this advertising space must attract them and sell them.

The following exercise will help you focus your manuscript on the needs of your audience so you will be able to slant the book toward them.

Only when you have polished your back cover copy should you begin to write the book. Post your back cover worksheet on the wall in front of your keyboard and look at it often. Now all you have to do is deliver on all your promises.

Back covers of Dan Poynter's *The Self-Publishing Manual* **and Mindy Bingham's** *Choices.*

Use the following guidelines to draft your back cover advertising copy. The back cover worksheet indicates proper placement.

1. First you need an arresting headline addressed to potential buyers so they can relate to the book and find themselves in it. In the case of *CHOICES: A Teen Woman's Journal for Self-awareness and Personal Planning*, the buyer is not the teenager but the adult. The headline, then, is directed to the adult. The copy that explains why this book is important is directed to adults in terms they can relate to.

2. Sales copy. Concisely state what the book is about. What will the reader gain by reading this book? In the case of *The Self-Publishing Manual* the cover recommends that all authors read this book even if they do not plan to self-publish. The manuscript is written to give good inside information on the workings of publishing, to provide a good understanding of both the author's and publisher's side of the industry.

3. Make the author look like the ultimate authority on the subject. Unless you are a politician or a movie star—someone easily recognizable—your photo will not sell books. Avoid the ego-trips and use this space more effectively.

4. Testimonials and endorsements. Your book is not written yet so make up what you would like others to say about your book. Use names recognizable in your field—names that might impress buyers.

5. End with a sales closer in bold type. Ask the reader to buy the book.

6. Price. Pick a price you would like the book to sell for. What are the prices of other books in the field?

7. ISBN is an identification number. Do not worry about the International Standard Book Number just now.

1.

2.

4.

4.

4.

3.

5.

7.

6.

Back cover worksheet

WHAT SHOULD I TITLE MY BOOK? Start with a descriptive working title. You may change the title many times before the book is done but you want to select something now. Early selection gives you plenty of time to live with the title, to try it out on others. Often we are so close to our title that we fail to see it is not descriptive.

The purpose of your title is to attract attention, describe the contents and create interest. A title should:

1. Grab the attention of the bookstore browser
2. Clearly indicate the subject of the book
3. Limit the scope of the coverage

A good title can sell 15 percent more books. A poor title may "lose" the book and keep it from reaching its intended audience.

- **Same key word as subject.** Check *Books in Print* (you did save those photocopies from the library, didn't you?). If possible, the first word of the **title** should be the same as the **subject** to make the book easy to find. The book will be listed in *BIP* by title, author and subject. If the title and subject are the same, you have doubled your exposure. Most other directories list **only titles** in alphabetic order; position your book where it can be found.

Dan Poynter's parachuting titles all begin with the same key (subject) word:

> *Parachuting, The Skydiver's Handbook*
> *Parachuting Manual with Log*
> *Parachuting Instructor/Examiner* Course
> *Parachuting Manual for Square/Tandem Equipment*
> *Parachute Rigging Course*
> (The) *Parachute Manual*

Remember that computer searches are made on "key" words. Directories do not count "the" as a word in the alphabetical listings. A book entitled "Introduction to Parachuting" would be found under "I" in most directories.

- **Grab attention and make a promise**. Good book titles are the best teaser copy in both a magazine ad and on the bookstore shelf.

  Some words grab more attention than others. Hong Kong, Singapore, or Haiti suggest foreign intrigue. Casino, yacht, and diamonds suggest wealth. Can you think of words to suggest mystery, laughter, romance, fantasy, violence? What do these words suggest: ravish, cuddle, beauty, scar, tickle? Which title would sell more books: "Three Days" or "Three Nights"? It is amazing what image you can produce with a few words.

  Many books are sold by mail. To be marketed they must be advertised. Here the title must grab the attention of the reader and be descriptive enough so the consumer does not need to look at the book before deciding to purchase it.

  Think about your title and come up with a good "one liner" which tells a complete and compelling story. Spend as much time and effort as you would selecting a name for your first born child. The title is the single most important piece of promotional copy you will write for your book.

- **Scope**   Is your book a guide, complete, treatise, new, manual, or handbook?

- **Character**   Is this an academic work, technical volume, popular book?

- **Image**   Does the title project an image making the book magnetic or repulsive?

> Drinking and Driving is no Accident, How to Avoid
> Becoming a Victim *were the title and subtitle of Robert*
> *Penkivich's new book. The problem is that while everyone is*
> *against accidents and no one wants to be a victim, the subject*
> *is unpleasant. With that subtitle, few people would read the*
> *book or even buy it. So Bob changed the title to* Drinking
> and Driving is no Accident, The Inside Story. *The book*
> *is the same, only the title is different.*

- **Do not mislead.** Did you know *What Color is Your Parachute*
  is about how to find a job? If you work in personnel, you
  are familiar with the term "golden parachute"; if you don't,
  you are not. Was the film *Chariots of Fire* about running in
  the Olympics or the burning of Rome? Is *Whack on the Side*
  of the Head a humor book or is von Oech trying to change
  your way of thinking?

  Fiction titles may sometimes be cute or clever, nonfiction titles have to be descriptive. Clearly indicate the subject of your book.

  Use a dictionary and a thesaurus. Avoid large words
  and fuzzy definitions. Try the titles out on friends. Do they
  know what the book is about?

  The words should be easy to remember and easy to
  say—they should relate well to each other. A short title is
  best because it is easier for a customer to remember.

  Titles must read well and be grammatically correct.
  Do not use abbreviations or symbols/words such as H_2O
  that cannot be easily read. For hydrochloric acid, would
  you look for the book under hyd or HCL? If people are
  confused by a title, they will not ask for it.

- **Title length**   The title should be the fewest possible words
  that adequately describe the contents of the book. Make
  the title short, clear, current, specific, familiar, colorful and
  catchy: one to six words.

THE SUBTITLE should be longer and provide more description. Since *Books in Print* and most other book directories do
not describe the books, your title and subtitle must do the
job.

COMPUTER SELECTION GUIDE, Choosing the Right Hardware & Software: Business-Professional-Personal is listed under the most common heading "computers" while the rest of the title and subtitle tell what the book is about.

There isn't any limit to the length of subtitles but if yours is too long, it may be abbreviated in the listings. Most listings are computerized today and the programs only allocate so many characters to book titles/subtitles.

A WORKING TITLE gives you a name to call the book while you are preparing it. Many people get in the habit of just calling their manuscript "the book." Psychologically a working title makes the manuscript feel much more alive.

Mindy Bingham had a bestseller in Choices, a Teen Woman's Journal for Self-awareness and Personal Planning *but the schools needed a companion boys' edition. The working title for the new book began as* Son of Choices, *then* Choices II *or* Choices Too *and later* Changes. *Only after considerable market testing revealed that men reacted negatively to "changes" did she come up with* Challenges.

Do not get hung up on the title if it just does not come to you right away. Although many books are started with a great title (like this one. . . we constantly had people coming up to us at parties to tell us about 'the book inside them' and asking for advice on how to write a book) most authors do not settle on a final title until the manuscript is nearly completed.

COPYRIGHT While the text of books can be copyrighted, the title cannot. There are just too many books and not enough words. Check *Books in Print* and find a combination of words which do not compete with another recent book. Use generic rather than proprietary names, which may be trademarked.

NEXT make up a list of possible titles and try them on your friends and associates. Show them a title and ask them what they think the book is about. How do they react? Do they perk up? Record reactions. Big corporations spend lots of money testing names for new products. Make sure your friends are being objective and not agreeing with you just to be nice. A good title is one that gives you that "yeah!" feeling. A good title is one that sells the book.

"Give me a condor's quill! Give me Vesuvius' crater for an ink-stand!. . . To produce a mighty book, you must choose a mighty theme."
- Melville

6

WHAT WILL YOUR BOOK LOOK LIKE?

YOUR NOTEBOOK To help you visualize your book, lay it out in a binder. This is like framing a house before adding the interior decoration. The finishing work will be easier and more fun once you can see where you are going. Find a large 3-inch, three-ring binder and place a label on the cover with your name, address, telephone number and a plea for the binder's return if lost.

   Make a page for each of the sections listed in this chapter and fill in as much information as you now have. Keep adding as you progress. The collected information does not yet have to be neat; the important thing is that now you have a place to store your material. As you add pages, as the book fills up, you will have more work to carry with you. When you find a few idle moments, open the book, draft and revise it, bit by bit. Tighten your writing, change words, cut out those which fail to add to your message. Revise and improve.

PARTS OF A BOOK Most books are divided into three main parts: preliminary pages or "front matter," the text and the "back matter."

"The entire industry is between the writer's thoughts and what the reader sees on the page." - Writers Connection.

Pull four or five different types of books off your shelf and compare them as you read further about each part of the book. Older hardbound books usually followed convention.

There are two pages to each sheet or leaf of paper. The "verso" pages are on the left-hand side and are even numbered while the "recto" pages are opposite.

THE FRONT MATTER is that material placed at the beginning of the book. It includes everything up to the start of Chapter One.

END PAPERS may be plain or printed, are usually of heavier paper, and are glued to the inside front and back covers of a hardbound (casebound) book. They hold the book together. Your binder will not require end papers.

TESTIMONIALS and other sales copy are being seen more and more on the first page of softcover books. This is important sales material. Think about the endorsements and testimonials you might like to have.

THE HALF-TITLE or bastard title is often the first printed page found in hardbound books. It contains only the title and it is a right-hand page.

There was a time when books were produced and sold without covers; it was up to the buyers to have the books bound if they wished. The half title page served to protect the title page and to identify the volume. The custom of including a half title page persists even though the original reason for it no longer exists.

THE FRONTISPIECE is a photograph found on the reverse of the bastard title page. Often this page is left blank instead or it is used more economically to list other books by the same author.

"A book is like a garden carried in a pocket. "- Chinese proverb

THE TITLE PAGE is on the right-hand side and lists the full title of the book with its subtitle if it has one. This page may also include the name of the author or editor, the publisher, whether this is an original or revised edition, and the year.

PEN NAMES seem to be a major preoccupation with new writers. There are few good reasons for changing your name when you write. If you are writing porno books, do not want your boss to know you are moonlighting or wish to conceal your sex (readers seem to prefer female names on romance novels), you might have a reason. But pen names spread you too thin and confuse your readers. As you write, you will establish a following. Using more than one name means establishing a readership for each. If your work is not good enough to sport your name, is the material good enough to print? It may be better to spare the tree.

If you do select a nom de plume, make sure it is not being used by another writer. Check the directories in the reference section of your public library.

Some authors use only their first and middle names as pen names while others select a maiden name or other family name.

Authors using a pseudonym must decide how they want their copyright handled. Should the book be registered in the pen name or the publisher's name? Listing the book in your name will give you away.

THE COPYRIGHT PAGE or "title page verso" is on the reverse of the title page and is the most important. Here you print the copyright notice (circle "c", year and name of copyright holder), indicate the printing history (number of printings and revisions), the ISBN, the Library of Congress Cataloging in Publication Data (including the Library of Congress Catalog number), name and address of the publisher and "printed in the United States of America" (to avoid export complications).

"If we encounter a man of rare intellect, we should ask him what books he read." - Ralph Waldo Emerson

Those who know the trade will turn to the copyright page first when picking up a book. Next to the cover, this page is the most important in selling a book, so make it complete.

COPYRIGHT is the subject which most interests potential authors. They want to know how to protect their precious material from others and to know how much of the other's work they can use.

A copyright covers exact printed words, not ideas or thoughts, so you are safe if you just do not copy word-for-word. The copyright law was completely rewritten in 1978 and it will be many years before every aspect of it has been interpreted by the courts. The courts seem to deal with each case individually when determining infringement. One test has been whether the original work is any less saleable once it has competition from an alleged infringer. Make it a rule never to copy any three words in a row. If your book is not recognizable as being a copy, you should be safe.

A copyright in your name is good for your lifetime plus fifty years (for co-authors, fifty years after the death of the last survivor). If you write a book for an employer (a "work for hire"), the copyright runs 75 years.

YOUR COPYRIGHTED MATERIAL is valuable property, or it may be one day. File copyright forms on all those magazine articles you do not get paid for. You may need an article for inclusion in a book someday and the expenditure on fees will confirm your profession to the IRS.

If you are asked for permission to reprint some of your work, you might allow a reprint of just a section or two, with a stipulation that an editor's note indicate it was used with your permission and came from your book. This will make you look more like an expert and is good publicity for the original work. A copyright on your book is not only for protection, it is prestigious; it shows you are a professional. For more information on copyrights, see the discussion in *Writer's Market* and read John McHugh's *Permission, Copyright and Fair*

Use: A Guide for Book Publishing Managers and the other copyright references listed in the Appendix.

THE DEDICATION PAGE usually contains a short statement but some authors like to praise their friend(s) in great detail. It is not likely that anyone other than the person mentioned will care about the dedication.

For Rachel and Jonathan,
my dear friends and advisers in the art of living

To W.H.Y.H.,
who taught us both,
among many other things,
that publishing is more
than a business.

To Fritz,
without whom this would have been
an address book.

Remembering TINA and JAY—
With Love

To our families,
whose patience made
this book possible

TO BETTY

A search of the books on your shelf will reveal that most books are dedicated to a spouse—the person who put up with the author during the agony (for them both) of writing. This right-hand page was used historically by writers to acknowledge their patrons: the person or institution that supported them during the writing.

THE EPIGRAPH PAGE contains a pertinent quotation which sets the tone of the book. Using a separate page for an epigraph in most books is a waste of space.

THE TABLE OF CONTENTS should start on the right-hand side. This page will include the chapter numbers, chapter titles and beginning page numbers. Remember, when buying technical, professional or how-to books, most people turn immediately to the Table of Contents to check the coverage. Consider this when you name your chapters.

A LIST OF ILLUSTRATIONS is in order if the book is heavily illustrated or if it is a picture-type book. Usually this page is a waste of space. The same goes for a list of tables, especially if they are tied directly to the text.

THE FOREWORD is positioned on the right-hand side and is a pitch for the book by someone other than the author. The name of the contributor appears at the end. Think about who you might get to write this endorsement. Try to find someone well-known in your field. If you include a foreword, note the correct spelling; it is not "forward."

THE PREFACE is written by the author and tells why and how he or she wrote the book. It appears on the right-hand side. If you have an important message and want to be sure the reader receives it, put it in Chapter One, not in the preface or introduction.

ACKNOWLEDGMENTS are a great sales tool. List everyone who helped you in preparation of your manuscript. People love to see their name in print and each one will become a disciple, spreading the word on your great contribution to literature. They may even purchase a copy. Record names of contributors as you encounter them so that you do not forget anyone. If you list contributors in alphabetical order, they will be less concerned where they appear on the list.

"I am a part of all that I have read." - John Kiern

THE INTRODUCTION tells who the book is intended for and how the reader should use it.

THE LIST OF ABBREVIATIONS is only required in some very technical books.

THE REPEATED BASTARD TITLE is next, is optional and is a waste of space.

DISCLAIMERS are showing up in more and more books today. See the one in this book as an example.

Obviously, if all the front matter pages listed above were included in your book, you would have a number of pages already. You do not need all these pages and it is recommended that you do away with most except the title page, copyright page, acknowledgments and table of contents.

THE TEXT of the book is the meaty part on which the front matter and back matter hang. This is the second or main section. Most of the rest of this book concerns the text of your book.

DIVISIONS are sometimes made in long books with distinct but related sections. Their title pages contain the name and number of the section and their reverse sides are usually blank.

CHAPTERS are used to divide the book into sections, each covering a different aspect of the subject.

CHAPTER TITLES should reveal the subject of the chapter to aid the reader in finding what he or she wants. The reader may be skimming the book in a store pending possible pur-

---

"There is more treasure in books than in all the pirates' loot on Treasure Island... and the best of all, you can enjoy these riches every day of your life." - Walt Disney

chase or may be referring back to something he or she read. In either case, you want the description to be as clear as possible.

THE CHAPTER SUBHEAD or paragraph head is a secondary heading or title, usually set in less prominent type than the main heading, to divide the entries under a subject. Subheads can contribute a logical progression, aid in finding needed material and help to break up long chapters.

FOOTNOTES are not needed except in technical publications. If your book will be used as a research tool, the readers may want the footnotes to follow up on the material. Where footnotes must be used, some people recommend they be placed at the end of the chapter or in the appendix as it is more time consuming and therefore costly to place them at the bottom of each page.

THE BACK MATTER is all that reference material such as the glossary and index placed at the back of the book. It is less expensive to revise lists at the end of the book when reprinting; try not to print lists subject to change in the text.

THE APPENDIX contains important charts, graphs, lists, etc. and it may be composed of several sections. It is permissible to set this reference material in smaller type. The appendix begins on a right-hand page.

THE ADDENDUM has brief, late additional data. It is printed as part of the book or on a loose sheet.

ERRATA are errors discovered after printing. The list is printed on a separate sheet and may be pasted in or loose.

AUTHOR'S NOTES come next and include additional information in chapter order.

THE GLOSSARY is an alphabetically arranged dictionary of terms peculiar to the subject of the book. Some authors like to save space by combining the glossary and the index. Others define terms in the text as they are encountered. The glossary begins on a right-hand page.

THE BIBLIOGRAPHY lists the books you used in writing your book. Some authors place the bibliography at the end of each chapter. When at the end of the book, the references may be in appearance order or arranged by subtopic.

THE AFTERWORD is sometimes seen in manuals. Often it is a personal message from the author to the reader wishing the best of luck and/or requesting suggestions for revisions.

COLOPHON is Greek for "finishing touch" and details the production facts by listing the type style, designer, typesetter, printer, kind of paper, plate maker, binder, etc. It is not as common as it once was but is used more and more today in special "labor of love" type publications.

THE INDEX aids the reader in locating specific information in the pages and is particularly important in reference works. Many librarians will not purchase books without indexes. Assembling the index is time consuming unless you have a word processor, and the index must be revised every time the book is updated because the page numbers change. The index begins on a right-hand page. It should be positioned near the very end of the book to make it easy to locate.

ORDER BLANK   The last page of the book should contain an offer for more books and a coupon; place it on a left-hand page—facing out. Some readers will want to purchase a copy for a friend while others may want a copy for themselves after seeing your book at a friend's home or in the library. Make ordering easy for them. This coupon system works.

At Para Publishing, more orders are received on book order blanks than from the general brochure or any other single promotion.

Now that the outside of your book is organized, it is time to work on the inside.

"A good book has no ending." - R. D. Cummings

7

GETTING READY TO WRITE
Organization and Research

ORGANIZATION Many people want to "write a book." Most people have the ability, some have the drive but few have the organization. Therefore, the greatest need is for a simple system, a "road map." In Chapter Six we laid out the structure for your book. In this Chapter we will help you get organized.

You may be anxious to put your first words on paper, but important preliminary work remains to be done. The steps described in this chapter can make the difference between a rewarding authoring experience and a frustrating one; a well-thought out book and a poorly-produced manuscript. The basic organizational plan in this book will provide direction, promote drive and expose ability no one thought existed.

AFFIRMATIONS Most of the successful people in the world are people with positive attitudes. They are the people who give themselves the "I can" message. Affirmations are positive statements made to yourself that affirm your beliefs. Constant repetition will lead to their acceptance by the mind and establish them in your conscious and subconscious.

> *"The best time for planning a book is while you're doing the dishes."*
> - Agatha Christie

Sports psychology uses this technique for athletes. Think of the pole vaulter going for a new height. The athlete will stand at the beginning of the runway and repeat to himself "I can go over the top." You need to go through the same process as you begin your project. Begin by making affirmations to yourself as you get up each morning and as you sit down to begin your project. Some statements you might use are:

"I can write this book."

"My idea for this book is a good one."

"I am in control of my book project."

"I understand how to follow through with my book project."

"I can be the successful author of a book."

"I can research this project extensively."

"I will be an author."

"My book will be published."

By repeating these or appropriate affirmations daily your subconscious will begin to accept them as truths and you will find it "easier" to take the appropriate action to achieve your goal.

SETTING GOALS that are measurable and have a timetable attached is another process used by successful people. When writing, it is easy to procrastinate. Goals and a timetable will help you stay on schedule and moving in the proper direction. Listing goals and objectives helps you break the project into smaller pieces, making it appear more manageable and realistic.

Just as you need a timetable, you need to be able to measure each step toward your goal. If your goal is very specific, objectives will often suggest themselves. If you want to lose 15 pounds in ten weeks, you will need to lose a pound and a half each week. If you want to write a first draft of 15 chapters in ten weeks, you will have to write an average of a chapter and a half each week.

If your goal is to complete the manuscript of a 10-chapter career counseling book for high school students in one year—some of your objectives might be:

- To spend 3 months on the preparation and research stage of the book.

- For the first draft, write one chapter per week.

- To locate six peer reviewers—two high school counselors, one business personnel director, one concerned parent and two high school students.

YOUR WRITING TIMETABLE You might like to adapt the following timetable to your own needs. After each objective write in a proposed completion date. This will help you see how you are doing. Adjust your plans and expectations if you are not able to keep up with this schedule.

Share this timetable with those close to you. You might even post it next to your mirror or on your home office door. But remember it is only a guide. Getting hung up on your deadlines might lead you to do an inferior or incomplete job. Stress stifles your creativity.

Your first responsibility as an author is to deliver clear concise and accurate information. Do not skimp in any of these areas just to meet a deadline. The timetable is to help you see how far you have come and how far you have to go.

Reward yourself when you finish each step. Great writers like Mark Twain, Dostoyevsky, Mencken and Dickens worked better under the pressure of deadlines. You probably will too. A complete timetable provides many incremental deadlines.

"They are able who think they are able." - Virgil

TIMETABLE FOR MANUSCRIPT GENERATION

	Projected completion date
INITIATION: GETTING STARTED	
Evaluate my motivation for writing my book	
Review my strengths and limitations and develop a plan	
INSPIRATION: BOOK IDEA	
Research the competition and marketability of my topic	
Visualize the book and write the back cover copy	
Negotiate writing time and space with my self and my family	
Make the decision to go ahead with my project	
Write my timetable	
PREPARATION: RESEARCH	
Set up binder	
Set up work area	
Gather all books and magazines related to my topic	
Write for further information	
Complete the outline of my book	
Organize my material with the "pilot system".	
Locate any collaborators needed	

	Projected completion date
*If you wish to approach a traditional publisher, now is the time to send a query letter.	
PERSPIRATION: WRITING	
Complete first rough draft of book	
Make list of needed photos and drawings	
Content edit	
Conduct more research to fill in the gaps	
Interviews	
Complete second draft(s)	
VERIFICATION: FINAL EDITING FOR ACCURACY	
Send chapters to experts (peers) in field for technical review	
Complete third draft	
Send manuscript to copy editor for punctuation and grammar review	
Complete fourth draft	
PUBLICATION: PRODUCTION AND PROMOTION	

*At this point your objectives will depend on the publishing route you choose. See Chapters Sixteen and Seventeen.

PRODUCTION RATE Good organization prevents writing blocks. A good system prevents procrastination. Set realistic deadlines of so many sections or pages or words per day. It may be helpful to have a friend or family member who will hold you accountable. A regular routine creates momentum—which encourages writing. Without continuity in your writing schedule, you must rebuild momentum each time you sit down to create. When you reach major milestones, give yourself a small reward. You will get a tremendous feeling of pride and accomplishment when you are just a little ahead of schedule.

VISUALIZATION Another powerful psychological tool is visualization. Sit down and think what your book will look like. Consider the cover, weight, thickness, the colors, the sales copy on the back cover, etc. See your book in your mind. Imagine holding your book and looking at it. When you visit a bookstore (if that is where you think your book might sell) go to the section where the book would be displayed and visualize your product there with your name on the spine.

Sometimes it helps to have the cover art completed at the beginning of the project. Even a rough sketch of your cover idea hanging over your typewriter or word processor can be motivating and it helps you press on with the project.

> *The cover art for* Challenges *was completed before 20 percent of the text was written. The artist, Robert Howard, interviewed Mindy for nearly two hours about the theme and the feeling of the text. The art captured the spirit of the book so well that it gave Mindy and her co-authors the inspiration to push on to complete the manuscript.*

Your mental picture of your book may change as you progress with the manuscript. But by forming a mental image of your future book, you have already begun to realize your goal.

> *"Writing is a solitary occupation. Family, friends, and society are the natural enemies of the writer. He must be alone, uninterrupted, and slightly savage if he is to sustain and complete an undertaking."* - Lawrence Clark Powell.

ORGANIZE YOUR WORKSPACE The successful home office workspace is the result of careful attention to space, furnishings, storage and equipment. You should locate the workspace where you will be undisturbed, comfortable and close to your writing tools.

Set up a writing sanctuary in a spare room, wall unit, closet or a corner of the living room. Keep all your writing materials and research tools there. Your creative writing time is precious; do not waste it in setting up your work area each day.

FINDING TIME Time or lack of it is the most frequently heard excuse for not writing. But somehow you always find the time for those things most important to you. Just put them first. Often you can fit in an hour of writing time each day by completing other chores faster. Or you might get up one hour earlier each day. This has definite advantages, since the house is quiet, the telephone does not ring and the early morning is one of the most creative and productive times for most writers. Once you gather momentum in your project, you will find it easy to get up early; you won't even miss that hour of sleep. View writing as a serious job. Use discipline. You must put this hour first and not let anything or anyone interfere with it. The affirmation 'Right now my book is my priority. I will work on it (#) hours per day,' may help you stay on track.

How much time do you spend watching television, eating out, talking on the telephone, browsing in stores, or socializing with people you do not really enjoy? Why not use some of this time for your project? There are 8,760 hours in a year. Surely you can allocate some of them to your writing project.

Bargain with your family for uninterrupted time. Just one interruption can blow your concentration for twenty minutes—and ruin your day. It is difficult to pick up where you left off.

> *"If my doctor told me I had only six months to live, I wouldn't brood. I'd type a little faster."* - Isaac Asimov

BEST TIME OF DAY TO WRITE Write when you are the most creative. For some authors, this means getting up early. Others write better in the evening. It does not matter when you write as long as you write regularly during your most creative period each day without interruption.

Set up a schedule and try to write at least one hour each day. Writing less or taking off for too many days between creative periods will force you to waste time refreshing your memory.

RESEARCHING YOUR SUBJECT will fill in the gaps in personal experience. Research is simply reading, interviewing, making notes and rearranging the gathered pertinent information. The craft of nonfiction writing is based upon research. Most kinds of fiction require research, as well. The best research usually comes from original sources such as diaries, historical societies, letters, journals, old newspaper files and on-the-spot observation. Here are several ways to find the information you need.

Researchers   If you do not have the time to do all the required research, it is possible to hire someone to do it for you. But good research is detective work. One fact may lead to another idea so it is best to do most research yourself. However, researchers can be helpful when you have to find specific information that might require time you don't have.

Library   The importance of using the library cannot be over-emphasized. All research must begin there and most of the required information will be found within its walls. But there are different types of libraries and each has specific kinds of references. You won't find much fiction in a college library. Law libraries have every law book you are likely to need—and not much else. The public library may cover more subjects, but only lightly because it must serve the general public. Generally, you will find three important sources of information there:

"Writing is the art of applying the seat of the pants to the seat of the chair." - Mary Heaton Vorse

1. The card catalog listing all its books by title, author and subject. Most libraries have abandoned the cards in favor of microfilm. The listings are viewed on readers.

2. Indexes such as the *Reader's Guide,* catalogs of articles, essays, reports and other information.

3. General references such as encyclopedias, dictionaries and directories.

Be a detective. When you run out of leads, ask the librarian. Libraries carry hundreds of indexes, listings and source books. Gather everything ever written on your subject. Load yourself up with so much material you will have to decide what to leave out. Overdo it and you can be proud to know that you have covered the subject completely.

Borrow from the library or purchase all the recent magazines in your subject area. Tear out or photocopy all the important articles and underline their most important parts. Always write the name of the periodical and the issue date at the top of the page so you know the origin of the article and how old the information is.

Find all the recent books on your topic and buy them or get them from the library. Check *Books in Print* for books currently available. Comb used-book stores for older books. Most books should be purchased and added to your personal library. (While shopping in the used-book store, pick up references such as a thesaurus and a style manual. A few years old, they are much cheaper and still perfectly good.)

Some books and magazines in the library will be restricted to the reference room. When you cannot check them out, make notes of small bits of information and use the photocopy machine to record longer pieces. Be sure to have rolls of coins because many libraries have a limit on the amount of change they will give. If you wish to use photos and drawings of material with expired copyrights, use a plain paper photocopier for the drawings and reshoot the photos with a

---

"History does not repeat itself. Nonfiction writers repeat each other."

camera (more on this later). Even if the copyright has not expired, make a photocopy of valuable illustrations to guide you in your research. Photocopy useful parts of checked-out books and magazines at the local copy center. They will have a plain paper copier and usually charge less than the library.

Make good use of your library time by bringing along a list of questions to be answered. Do not get sidetracked with recreational reading.

Write for information. After exhausting the library's information, move on to the many other available sources.

Read through the magazines in your field and send to every pertinent advertiser for more information on their products. Many will supply you with valuable information on the product area. Use the quick order "bingo" cards in the magazines and write short requests to the rest. Later you may write to people and companies for more specific information. Right now you are just fishing.

Send for *Selected U.S. Government Publications* to the Superintendent of Documents, USGPO, P.O. Box 1821, Washington, DC 20402. This is a monthly catalog of government publications. Many of these pamphlets are also available at U.S. Government bookstores in the larger cities. Check the white pages.

University Microfilms (300 North Zeeb Road, Ann Arbor, MI 48106) has over 150,000 doctorial dissertations in every field. They can run a computer search on any key word and provide a list of papers in which that word appears. Then you may order copies of the dissertations you want.

Tapping distant data bases with a computer is covered in the Tools Chapter.

Many documents are not copyrighted.   Normally you will be gathering material, blending it together, boiling it down and extracting information of interest to your specific group of readers. However, there will be times when you find a

PARA PUBLISHING

Books by Dan Poynter

June 1, 1985

High Tech Books, Inc.
Promotion Department
454 Silicon Street
Cupertino, CA 95014

Ladies and Gentlemen:

Your book, <u>Ghostwriting</u> <u>For</u> <u>Fun</u> <u>and</u> <u>Profit</u> by Carolyn Porter, has been recommended to us as a resource which should be listed in our new book on methods for writing books. To be considered for inclusion, please send the following:

1.   A review copy of the book (hurt copies are acceptable.)
2.   The current list price.
3.   Ordering information (bookstore or mail order address.)
4.   A book description in 200 words or less (a brochure is acceptable.)
5.   Photocopies of at least two independent reviews.

Para Publishing has a growing line of writing/publishing resource books. We expect the audience for this new book to be quite large. Any book mentioned in the text should experience a number of sales.

We are working under a very tight schedule. Please give this request your immediate attention.

Sincerely,

PARA PUBLISHING

Daniel F. Poynter
Publisher

DFP/ms

Post Office Box 4232 ——— Santa Barbara, CA 93103 USA——— Telephone: (805) 968-7277

The letter used for this book.

piece of material you simply must have. If you want to determine whether some material is protected under either the current or pre-1978 law, the Copyright Office will conduct a search for you. Send them as much information as possible, such as the author, title, publisher and publication date. The cost is $10 per hour and they should be able to make two searches per hour. Government and military publications are in the public domain. Even if they were not, they would probably be covered by the Freedom of Information Act. If you really need a piece of material, military or civilian, ask for permission. It is safer and cheaper than hiring a lawyer later to prove you have a right to it.

A good way to make your request for permission to use someone's copyrighted material is to photocopy the material you want to use, circle just that part, and send it to the copyright holder, along with a letter explaining how you want to use the material and asking for a release. Be sure to ask for the world rights to reprint the material in case your book is picked up by a foreign publisher. Wait until you receive a reply in writing before you proceed with publishing. Sometimes you will not be granted permission or the price will be very high. Also the copyright holder may require you to note the source and that permission was given.

The Yellow Pages and the telephone often uncover a great wealth of information. You can always find someone with information or a lead to information.

Attend instruction courses at a local college. Keep up with the latest technology. Find out what is on the mind of the other students—and answer their questions with your book.

Press pass Now that you are researching, you are a member of the print media and will be able to attend a lot of related events free. When visiting trade shows, use your new business card to get a press pass, media packet and preferential treatment.

Interviews with the experts will uncover inside details and current information. In most nonfiction book writing, interviews are used to fill in the gaps. As you draft your book, questions should be written in the margin and then transferred to a separate sheet.

You may write or call the expert. Make an appointment so your interviewee will be relaxed and will have the calendar cleared for you. Identify yourself and your project so the person understands who you are and what you want. Be prepared. The interview will go smoother and faster if you have a list of specific questions. Formulate your questions so they cannot be answered with a straight "yes" or "no." Make your expert explain or qualify his or her answers. Check the questions off as you proceed through the interview. Some answers will lead to further questions.

Do not talk about yourself during the interview unless you are asked. You won't learn if you are talking. One of your major missions in an interview is to make a friend or acquaintance of your contact. He or she is a resource and you may wish to call back later for more leads or verification of facts.

OUTLINE your book so you can see where you are going. This is one of the most important steps in the production of your material, so take your time and give it a lot of thought. A carefully thought-through outline will save you a lot of work later when you start writing your first draft. It will help clarify what kind of research you need to do. It is another tool to help keep your project on track.

Make up a list of chapters and note what you plan to cover in each. Some authors like to place each chapter on a different card so the cards may be arranged and rearranged.

This project may take from a couple of days to a couple of months. Once you have completed the first draft of your outline set it aside for a while so you can mull it over. You want it to be complete, ordered and as close to the final outline of the book as possible. The more complete and ordered your outline, the easier it will be to write the first draft.

"If you don't know where you're going, you're there."

ORGANIZE YOUR MATERIAL WITH THE "PILOT SYS-TEM." Sort all your research material and "pile it" as required. Decide on your chapter titles and, using scissors, tape and staples, sort all this copied material into the applicable chapter piles. During your library research, you must have written down a number of interesting observations, many of your own experiences. Add your own notes to the piles. Laying out the piles is fun. You are only getting ready to work and this layout makes the big job look like many small jobs.

Now take the papers from your "horizontal filing cabinet" and spread out the individual chapters. The piles will probably completely fill the living room. Pick an interesting pile, any one, not necessarily the first, and go through it, underlining important points and writing in your additional comments. Write out longer thoughts on a tablet and file them in order in the pile.

This floor spread will enable you to see the whole inter-related project, lending excitement and encouragement—a great incentive. Move the piles around to insure a good, logical flow of thought and to avoid duplication of copy. Discard bad and duplicate material.

This use of information from other sources is not plagiarizing; it is research. Your notes insure that you will not leave out any important points. However, you will be entertained as you compare what various authors say about the same item. The similarities are often remarkable. You will come across the same words and phrases time and again.

IMPROVE THE MATERIAL by continually reviewing it and boiling it down. As you read what others say on a particular point, your memory will be jogged. You will have additional points, a clearer explanation or an illustrative story.

Keep your mind tuned-in to your subject. Stay alert to information which may be useful. Write it down and date the scrap of paper. Be thorough! Consider what will be on the reader's mind and answer those questions in convincing detail.

"Writers often say, truthfully, that they are as much at work away from their desks as in the act of writing itself." - Paul Horgan

Use imagination in writing, not in research. Be accurate. Just because you find some information in print, do not assume it is correct. Double check all facts—do not perpetuate a myth. You are about to commit history—it is a great responsibility. If you disagree with another author, you can always say "some people believe. . ." and then tell it your way. You have the advantage of the most recent information since you came last.

Carry paper and pen with you at all times, especially when working, running or engaging in any solo activity. This is the time to think, create, compose; this is when there is no one around to break your train of thought. Some authors keep a pad or tape recorder in their car and compose while commuting. When you are confined, captive, isolated, you have nothing else to do but create. Make use of any available time. A lot of good material develops while attending dull meetings.

Some people like to work with a small pocket tape recorder, but remember that someone must transcribe this noise onto paper. If you often dictate letters and have a secretary to transcribe your tapes, this may be the most comfortable and most efficient method for you.

When a particularly original thought or creative approach hits you, write it down or record it immediately or you will lose it. Keep on thinking and keep on note-taking. Add your thoughts and major pieces to the piles. Draw up a list of questions as they come to mind so that you will remember to conduct the research to answer them.

TEST YOUR MATERIAL with lectures, demonstrations, seminars and/or magazine articles. Gain experience and gain feedback from your audience. Adopt what works and modify what does not.

> *"After-all, most writing is done away from the typewriter, away from the desk. I'd say it occurs in the quiet, silent moments, while you're walking or shaving or playing a game, or whatever, or even talking to someone you're not vitally interested in. You're working, your mind is working, on this problem in the back of your head." - Henry Miller.*

The material for Choices, *grew out of a class taught in several Santa Barbara high schools. The exercises were developed and tested with the teenagers. If an exercise worked, it was added to the manuscript. If it didn't, it was thrown out.*

By now, you should be organized. You have begun your research and your project is taking on its direction. The next chapter offers some suggestions to help make the coming work easier and more rewarding.

"*I put a piece of paper under my pillow, and when I could not sleep I wrote in the dark.*" - Henry David Thoreau.

8

TOOLS OF THE TRADE

All you really need to create a book are paper and pencil. A desk with good lighting, typewriter, reference books and a filing cabinet will make the job easier. When you shop for equipment, buy the best you can afford. You will have them for some time and nothing is worse than a cheap tool which performs poorly or which breaks just when you need it. Plumbers have the best tools, so should wordsmiths.

Office machinery such as photocopy machines, tape recorders, word processors and cordless telephones have created a revolution in the process of gathering and writing information. The machines cut out the laborious, repetitive work and allow you to concentrate on the creative aspects of the writing project. You may not mind all the typing you do now but once you let a computer do your retyping you realize that secretarial tasks like this just take time away from your writing.

Major purchases of supplies and equipment should be made only after carefully reading *Office Purchasing Guide* by Tod Snodgrass, listed in the Appendix.

REFERENCE BOOKS Dictionaries and other reference books are available much more cheaply at used book stores. The books you should have are listed in Chapter Ten.

OFFICE FURNITURE, too, can be purchased much more cheaply second-hand.

We have discussed manual methods of writing a book. Now, since so many people have access to computers and other office machinery, we will describe their use in manuscript generation. Consider how the following items might be useful to you.

COPY MACHINE   The photocopy machine is a very useful tool for research. When setting off for the library in the search for information, always take a pocketful of coins for the copy machine. Photocopy the lists and other useful information you find rather than hand-copying them onto index cards. Use the same method when doing research at home. Build the information piles with these photocopied notes as described in Chapter Nine ("pilot system").

Of course, the copy machine is also useful for making duplicates of your manuscript. An extra copy of your work should always be stashed in a safe place. And you will need copies of sections of the manuscript to send off for peer review.

Use the local copy shop or purchase your own machine. Get out the Yellow Pages and look under "Copying & Duplicating." Call all the shops in your area to compare prices. Usually those shops situated near colleges are the most competitive.

Prices of machines have fallen tremendously in the last few years. If you decide to buy, consider only those machines commonly known as "dry toner, heat fusing, any paper copiers." These are the true "plain paper" copiers. If you are making copies on a daily basis, owning your own machine will pay for itself very quickly. Copies will be cheaper, you will save gas and, more important, you will save time. You will be able to work when you want to and this means you will finish book sections and other projects sooner.

YOUR TYPEWRITER or word processor is your most important piece of machinery; spend the money and get a good one. You are a "wordsmith" now and require the best word processing machine you can afford. If you choose a typewriter, the new electronic machines are less tiring to operate and they will make your work look better. They are easier to maintain, since they have fewer moving parts than electro-mechanical models. These machines can be used to create brochures and forms because of their clear, sharp type. There are a few electronic typewriters on the used machine market and there will be more now that offices are switching to computerized, video display text-editing equipment.

If you have to buy a new typewriter, consider paying for the machine over several months or years. After all, you will be using it over a long period. If you are already in a high tax bracket, you should consider leasing all your office equipment. The costs are tax deductible and you tie up less money. Ask your accountant.

Visit a store which carries a large variety of typewriters and compare them. Some of the new small electrics have a different feel than the IBM Selectric we all learned on. Make sure you like the feel of the keyboard.

COMPUTERS The computer is making writing a more attractive, affordable and competitive option in today's market. There is a lot of "electronic authoring" going on: many writers are using personal computers with word processing programs to generate book manuscripts. This one invention is prompting a veritable book explosion.

A word processor (or a personal computer with a word processing program) is an expensive typewriter but a very smart one. It is a typing system which allows instantaneous editing and it has an electronic memory capable of storing everything you type into it. The word processor saves time by eliminating both the retyping of previously approved text and redundant proofreading. Errors are caught and corrected during editing, and the machine keeps those phrases, paragraphs or pages error-free thereafter. Only corrections or additions need be proofed.

COMPUTER WRITING Computers improve writing immeasurably. There is a big difference between a manuscript written, edited and typed by hand, and one that has been worked over as many times as necessary to pull every last bit of creativity out of the prose and to wring out every redundant phrase or unnecessary word.

People who type original material on a computer usually find that their style improves. They can edit while they type, catch extra words, break up long sentences, and reword for clarity.

Word processing reduces procrastination. You can start a big project anywhere simply by entering random thoughts. Once you have something down on paper, you can go back and add, edit, or clean up your prose.

Books are much easier to write on a word processor. During the editing phase, sentences, whole paragraphs and even entire chapters will be moved as the text is organized and refined.

Some word processors will mark the revised portions of a document in the margin to indicate which sections need a second look. Then on the final printout, the revision marks are deleted. This feature is especially useful in lengthy manuscripts.

COMPUTER RESEARCH With a modem and a telephone line, a computer may be used to search distant databases for information. For example, you might want a printout of all the patents issued in a certain area. A search of the *PAT-SEARCH Database* might cost $20 to $70. That may sound like a lot, but compare it with what it would cost to visit a distant patent library and spend days making a physical search. Data bases exist on every conceivable subject. Small firms specializing in database searches are springing up everywhere. Check the Yellow Pages.

COMPUTER EDITING may be done on the computer screen before the manuscript is committed to paper. There are never any erasures or correction fluid blemishes. If even the smallest error is found, it is easy to make the change. Only when

> *"Good writing does not come from fancy word processors or expensive typewriters or special pencils or hand-crafted quill pens. Good writing comes from good thinking." - Ann Loring in Write and Sell Your TV Drama.*

the document is ready does the computer's printer put it on paper.

The words are rearranged on the screen and then the machine takes over to automatically type out the revised, error-free document. If there are further changes, they are easily added to the copy residing in electronic storage. A final printout is made automatically and without the tedious retyping of previously proofread and approved copy.

Many computers will help you correct spelling. One proofreading program will go through a 20-page document comparing it to its own 80,000-word dictionary in about five minutes. The program catches the misspelled words, transpositions and the narrow characters added or missing from the middle of long words that human proofreaders sometimes overlook. The value of a spelling program is easily demonstrated on old, conventionally produced documents. It is amazing how many typos the spelling program will locate in a book thought to be error-free.

The spelling correction feature not only produces better work, it may also save a great deal of time. The operator can type at rough draft speed without slowing to check spelling or worrying about transpositions.

The "search" feature makes finding a particular place in the manuscript easy. When you have a piece of information to enter and cannot find the right place fast enough on the paper printout copy, just let the machine find it.

"Search & replace" is a time saver which promotes consistency. Say, for example, that "California" and "CA" were used interchangeably throughout a 250-page manuscript. By touching just a few keys, the machine will find the form not preferred each time it occurs and replace it with the one preferred. The machine will open the spaces for the inserted material, reformat (rearrange) the page and retype the final draft. Whereas a proofreader might miss a "CA" here and there, the computer will not. The changes can be made accurately, quickly and inexpensively.

THE THRILL OF VICTORY—THE AGONY OF DELETE
Computer editing can be both easy and hazardous. Some-

times you make a change only to decide you like the original version better. Major editing changes should be made on a separate document—and added into the manuscript once approved.

Store your work often. There is nothing more frustrating than working on a whole chapter to find your computer has "eaten it."

When Mindy was working on the book Challenges, *there was one particular chapter that had her stymied. She could not figure which approach to take. After spending three days researching and reading— ZAP, THE INSPIRATION HIT. She raced to the computer and spent three hours banging out the chapter. She finished with a great feeling of accomplishment for she knew it was just right! She sighed in relief, pushed the button for review and was faced with a blank screen. In her intense concentration, she had forgotten to store the document.*

BOOK INDEXING is a snap with a computer. Gone are the index cards, alphabetizing and retyping. Just build your index as you read the final proof of the typeset book.

COMPUTER TYPESETTING   There are four ways to set type with a computer. The first is to draft and edit the text on a computer and then to communicate it to a typesetting company over telephone lines. The result is regular photo-composition type. Typically this saves 30-40 percent in costs and cuts down the time to set a 150-page book from several weeks to a couple of days. Call typesetters in your area and ask if they have this capability. This book was typeset this way. See the Colophon in the back for specifications.

The second way to set type is to communicate your text to a Xerox 9700 Electronic Printer. Call the Printing Systems Division of Xerox in El Segundo, California, for the address of the 9700 service bureau nearest you.

The third way is to use a laser printer with your Macintosh or other computer to layout your pages. This way is new and shows great promise as all work can be done in-house.

A good example of this typesetting method is *Breastfeeding Success for Working Mothers* by Marilyn Grams, M.D.

The fourth way to set type is to draft and edit the text on the computer and then set the type with the computer's own letter quality printer. With the proper software, most machines will produce proportionally spaced, right-justified, strike-on, camera-ready type similar to an IBM Composer. Spellbinder is one word processing program that works when combined with the IBM Personal Computer and the Diablo 630 printer with the Bold PS printwheel. The secret is to use a carbon single-strike ribbon and clay-coated repro or "Photomaster" paper.

Dan Poynter has used this method to write, edit and typeset seven books. For more information on paste-up, see Publishing Short Run Books. *For a detailed description of the typesetting process, See* Computer Selection Guide.

Not only will a computer speed up your book generation, it may be used for correspondence, mailing list maintenance, bookkeeping and typesetting. For more information on writing with a computer see *Word Processors & Information Processing*.

THE NEXT MOVE   With the advances in software for word processing most people can learn the basics of their program with 2 to 4 hours of instruction. So start with word processing and consider other computer uses later. Once you do learn to use the machine, you will never go back to a typewriter.

Unless you are doing heavy word processing only, buy a microcomputer with a word processing program. Dedicated word processors (no data processing functions), are showing up on the used market at competitive prices.

With an eye toward resale, it is recommended you purchase a computer with the MS-DOS operating system. This means buying IBM or IBM compatible. These machines will hold their value longer. Because many people are buying them, there is more software available and they are worth more when trading up.

When you figure in the money saved in typesetting, investment tax credits and the mechanization computers provide your business, these machines are really quite inexpensive.

Start by visiting a computer store for a demonstration of word processing programs. There are many, many programs available and some work better and/or faster than others. Have the store demonstrate the programs on your application. Take your work in and let them show you how their machine and software will run it. Your enthusiasm will grow once you see the capability of these machines. Get bids from several dealers before buying—prices can vary by 10-50 percent. For more information, read Chapter Seven in Tod Snodgrass's book, *Office Purchasing Guide.* It deals specifically with negotiating a machine purchase.

If you are writing your first book, you may not want to run out right away and invest in a lot of expensive machinery. But many people have these machines at home or have access to them through work or friends. Many public libraries have machines available, for rent by the hour. The use of a copy machine and computer can cut manuscript generation time dramatically. It will be worth your while to arrange access to them.

TAPE RECORDERS are useful for recording notes as well as for interviewing. These recorders may be hand-held, designed for dictation and some are even voice-activated. Some people carry these "note-takers" when they are doing their "thinking" about their books; to record thoughts and inspirations while they are fresh and exciting. If your most creative times seem to be during your drive to work each morning, a tape recorder is a much safer way to capture your ideas than jotting them down on a pad in rush-hour traffic.

As illustrated in the Jim Comiskey story in Chapter Twelve, your information may be recorded on a tape recorder if you speak slowly. If you tend to think in spurts or are used to a dictating machine, you may wish to invest in one of them.

It is a lot easier to use a tape recorder than pad and pencil when conducting interviews. The machine ensures that you have all the information recorded and you can review your tape for different sections of your book. Some people tend to open up more when you use a tape recorder instead of taking notes. If your interviewee is a fast speaker, note taking can be frustrating for you both. But also be sensitive to the person who is intimidated by a tape recorder. If you sense inhibition, turn off the recorder and go back to note-taking. Always ask the person you are interviewing for permission to record the conversation.

For interviewing over the telephone, pickups are available from stores such as Radio Shack. Some telephone answering machines such as the Code-A-Phone Model 2540 also have the ability to record two-way conversations. Be sure you have received permission to record the telephone conversation with your interviewee before proceeding.

CAMERAS If your manuscript requires pictures and you do not already have one, you will want to get a good camera with attachments and a book on how to use them. There are many types of cameras but the most popular and versatile is the single lens reflex (SLR). Many used models and accessories are available at your discount photo shop and SLRs have good resale value. If all your subjects are still, you can get by with a cheaper match-needle model. If you are shooting fast-moving people or objects, you may need a camera with automatic features and/or motor drive (aircraft mounts may dictate motor drives and a remote firing device too). Olympus has the fastest motor drive, (five shots per second) and that still is not fast enough to get a series of photos to show the windup and throw of a Frisbee disc. But it is fast enough for most subjects and allows you to keep your eye on the subject rather than pulling away to advance the film. Some good automatic cameras are the Olympus OM-4, Nikon FE2, Minolta X-700, Pentax Super Program, Ricoh XRP, Canon A-1 Program and the Konica C35-AF.

VIDEO TAPE RECORDERS Video tapes are becoming more important as a source of research material. Begin collecting a library of tapes about the subject you wish to write on. This visual stimulus can be a motivating tool when you sit down to write your first draft. Later when you are published you can use your video tape recorder to record your television interviews and live lectures. These tapes can be added to your marketing and promotion materials.

Do not send video tapes through the mail unless they are well-wrapped and will be hand-cancelled at the Post Office window.

MACHINERY As you do more writing, look for labor-saving machinery to multiply your efforts. Personal computers, photocopy machines, cordless telephones and postage meters will save you time. They are much better buys than an employee and you will find that with investment tax credits and depreciation, machines are not very expensive.

"If I had eight hours to chop down a tree, I'd spend six sharpening my ax." - Abraham Lincoln

9

HOW TO WRITE A BOOK

It is not our intention to teach you the mechanics of writing; there are far too many good books available on working with words. Some are listed in the appendix. However, this chapter outlines a proven writing system and reveals a number of inside tricks used by successful authors.

If you haven't already done so, you must decide where your talents lie and what parts of your project you want to perform by yourself. Are you an idea person or are you a writer? Do you enjoy writing or do you want to be a published author without the "pain" of writing? If you plan to do most of the writing yourself, try the following system. You may plan to hire help, but unless you are hiring a ghostwriter or contract writer, you will still do most of the organization of the project yourself. Read this chapter in order to understand the system and consider the organization.

WRITING THE BOOK YOURSELF Creating your own material is easy if you have a system; all it takes is organization and discipline. Following the system outlined below, creating copy becomes challenging fun and allows you to easily see the progress you are making—which is encouraging. This method may be of some help in writing fiction, but it was developed specifically for nonfiction.

"Work is the price you pay for money."

TO GET STARTED, STRIP your notes by cutting, sorting and taping. Take one chapter from your "pilot system" piles and lay the paper strips out in logical order. Connect the strips with Magic Transparent Tape. If your photocopies were made on a plain paper copier, you will be able to write on the tape as well as the paper when adding notes. When adding your thoughts, never write on the back of a piece of paper. You want to be able to lay out all your materials where you can see them.

If you have a word processor, you will still use this system for writing and editing but the process will be mechanized. If you are using a typewriter, type on 3-hole punched mimeo paper; it is substantial and inexpensive. The holes even help you to see when the bottom of the page is coming up in the typewriter; it comes quickly when you are double-spacing. Do not use erasable paper, the ink comes off on the hands. Type, do not hand-write. You will need a typed copy of your draft to better visualize your work. Typing will save you one complete step.

LAYOUT THE BINDER. Now that you are generating copy, you need a place to store it. Add divider cards to your binder corresponding to the chapters you have selected. Insert the rough typed pages as you complete them. They should be numbered by chapter and page. For example, "6-14" would be page 14 in Chapter Six. As the piles come off the floor, cross the desk and flow through the typewriter or word processor into the binder, you will gain a great feeling of accomplishment.

You must decide now whether secondary matter is of value or just window dressing. An index, appendix, bibliography or directory may add to the usefulness of the book or may cost more than they are worth to include. It depends on the subject and your treatment of it. But all these items should be decided upon early, so a running list can be maintained as you do your research. Remember, some books are composed of nothing but lists.

> *"If you want to be a writer, forget it. If you have to be a writer, you just might make it."* - Sidney Sheldon.

Soon you will have a partial manuscript, something tangible to carry around. This makes you feel proud and allows you to work on your manuscript away from home. If your book is short, you might collect all your material in the binder, bypassing the piles of notes.

It is wise to photocopy your manuscript periodically for storage in another location. If the fruit of your creativity were misplaced or destroyed in a fire, you would suffer both financially and emotionally.

WRITING from the pasted strips may be done with a tape recorder, typewriter or word processor. With practice you will learn to think, create and compose at the selected machine. Write as you speak; relax and be clear. Make notes where you are considering illustrations. Type the manuscript double-spaced as you would the final copy. Initiate good habits.

Read the whole pasted-up section to grasp the overall theme. Then boil the material down and use your own words. Think about the section and how you might improve the message. Can't you say it better with fewer words?

Do not just write from the strips sentence-by-sentence. That might be plagiarism. For organization, list the main points and rearrange the pieces. If you are having trouble with a section, arrange it as best you can and come back to it later. If you still cannot bring the message together with a few well-chosen sentences, you may have to call another expert for his or her explanation of the subject matter. If you cannot reach the colleague or are otherwise still having trouble with a section, put the pile back on the floor and pick up an easier, more interesting pile. Skip around.

You have selected your subject and your audience— do not lose sight of who you are writing for. Talk to your audience, follow your outline and make sure your manuscript says what you want it to say—completely but concisely.

Many books should start off with an "action" chapter. Like the introductory part of a speech, the beginning of a book should arouse readers and whet their appetite. Too many

> "Begin every story in the middle, The reader doesn't care how it begins, he wants to get on with it." - Louis L'Amour.

authors want to start from the "beginning" and put a history chapter first. Readers want to know where-to and how-to. Do not lose them in the first chapter.

Do not start to write with Chapter One—to do so makes book writing look like an impossible mountain climb (with you at the very bottom). Select the chapter pile that looks the easiest. It may be the smallest pile or the most interesting one. Once you have written it, take the next most interesting chapter and so on. Soon you will be passed the half-way mark. You will be encouraged and will gather momentum. Using this approach, you will probably find yourself writing the first chapter last. This is as it should be as the first chapter usually serves as an introduction. You cannot know what it should say until the rest of the work is drafted. Many authors wind up completely rewriting and reslanting the first chapter because they wrote it first.

Do not be concerned with your writing style the first time around. The important thing is to get your thoughts down. Often these first impressions are the best; they are complete, natural and believable. Later you will make corrections, additions and deletions. Major changes will require rewriting while minor corrections only need some proofing marks. Sentences and paragraphs will be added by cutting and pasting-in the new material. With your book set up in loose leaf binder form, it will be easy to add material.

As you type up the first draft and later as you review it, you will decide whole paragraphs are misplaced. Using three-hole punched paper and a binder, it is an easy matter to cut, move and paste material. With a word processor, you will be moving material back and forth from chapter to chapter with the touch of a button or two.

If you lack a certain piece of information, a number or fact, leave a blank space, put a note in the margin and go on. If you are using a word processor, type "***" and go on. The asterisks stick out in a manuscript and you can always conduct a "search" for them just to make sure you have filled in

---

"Don't get it right. Get it written, then get it right." - Goren George Moberg in *Writing in Groups.*

all the blanks. Do not lose momentum. Similarly, if you find yourself repeating material, make a note in the margin so you can compare it later with the sentences in the other location.

Remember, writing from notes is not plagiarism but solid, thorough research—an efficient system made possible by Xerox. Practically every non-fiction book is simply a repackaging and updating of existing material with the author's personal experience and prejudices incorporated.

Draft one complete section (often several paragraphs) at a time if possible. One chapter at a time is better. Most beginning authors must work at regular jobs and are able to devote only a short period each day to their writing. But the more time you can put into each piece of the book, the better, as there will be greater continuity, less duplication and clearer organization. If you can only do a small section at a time, try arranging the pieces in the evening, reviewing them in the early morning, thinking about them while commuting, and then type it all up when you arrive home.

If you can, take two weeks off from work, shut out all distractions and become totally involved in the manuscript. Do not pick up the mail or answer the telephone. Eat when hungry, sleep when tired and forget the clock except as a gauge of your pace. Keep up the pressure and keep on typing. Pace yourself at, say, one chapter per day. You should not have to force yourself to write but you do need organization and discipline.

After you have written a few books, you will find yourself making fewer changes in your original draft. In fact, if you are using an IBM Correcting Selectric typewriter, you will find yourself changing the type balls to indicate which type faces you want to use. If you are using a word processor, you may even enter typesetting codes for automatic typesetting. Incidentally, many writers say the hum of an electric typewriter or word processor—knowing the electricity is on—prompts them to work.

Do not throw out your materials once your draft is typed. Put them in a cardboard carton. Someone may ask where you

---

"There is no such thing as a publishable first draft." - William Targ

found a particular piece of information and you may wish to locate it.

WRITING STYLE   Before writing a magazine article, it is important to read several back issues to pick up that publication's style. The same technique works in writing a book. Begin your writing session by reading a few chapters by a writer you admire.

Writing is a communication art. You should not try to impress. Write as you speak, avoiding big words where small ones will do. Most people regularly use only 800-1,000 of the some 26,000 English words available to them. Use simple sentences and be precise in your selection of words. Vary sentence and paragraph length and favor the shorter ones. Try to leave yourself out of the copy: avoid the word "I."

Use action nouns and verbs. Help the reader draw a mental picture by introducing sight, sound, smell, touch and taste to your copy. Be precise. Avoid superlatives and overuse of adverbs and adjectives. Study newspaper writing and place the words you wish to emphasize at the beginning of the sentence. The important sentence should start the paragraph and the main paragraph should head the chapter.

Relax, talk on paper, be yourself. Explain each section in your own words as you would trying to help a friend who is new to the subject. Do not use contractions in your writing as you do in your speech as they're (there is one now) more difficult to read. "Which" and "that" can usually be left out to the benefit of the sentence. Keep your writing short. In magazine writing, you may be paid by the word but in book writing additional words have a way of costing you so, edit out the junk.

Like a speech, every paragraph should have a beginning, a middle and an end. Use smooth transitions from paragraph to paragraph to make your writing flow. The first sentence of the paragraph is called the "topic sentence"—stay with one subject per paragraph.

"Less is more." - Robert Browning

Use proper terms; do not start a new language. Steer away from highly technical language; you will only turn off your reader.

One technique for educating your readers is to use the proper term and then follow it with the more popular word in parentheses. Educating the reader as you progress through the book is preferable to making him or her stop and refer to a glossary.

Anticipate trends to keep your work up to date. Use metric and non-sexist terms wherever possible. Cookbooks in the United States may not be ready to switch to metric and books on printing will deal with 17 x 22 presses and 5½ x 8½ books for a long time, but many measurements may be avoided by using comparisons. For example, instead of telling a parachutist to prepare for landing at "30 feet," say "at tree top height." The comparison is clearer anyway.

As a published author you are considered an expert. Whether you are writing fiction or nonfiction, you must be accurate. You have a responsibility to find out what happened (or in fiction, what could have happened at that particular time and place).

Be a professional and give the readers their money's worth. Your material will be used by others in coming years and you will be quoted. If you are accurate now, you will not be embarrassed later by the written legend you have created.

Writing is hard work; it is an intellectual and emotional workout. Some authors enjoy the discipline writing requires but more have a greater appreciation for the results.

Move through your notes and reduce those piles of research materials to pages in your binder. The next step is to clean up what you have written: revise and edit.

STORYBOARDING For fiction writers, the process is slightly different. Instead of taping strips of paper together, you may want to use a storyboard.

> *"What a heavy oar the pen is, and what a strong current ideas are to row in."* - Flaubert.

Set up a system to keep track of what is going on in your novel (or story or play). Use a bulletin board with cards attached or a notebook such as the one we have described here.

A storyboard gives you a visual prop for your storyline. As your ideas are generated and the plot begins to take shape, your storyboard allows you the freedom to add and move events around, always being cognizant of chronological order. So when the idea for a great scene hits, you can figure out where to add it to the manuscript.

It is essential to keep track of your chronology, (what year is it? if the heroine was 15 when your story began, how old is she now?), the facts (if your story takes place in 1885, could there be a telephone in the house?), and the situation (was George at the fateful meeting, or did you place him in Siberia at the time it took place?).

You will find it helpful to have something to refer to when the action gets heavy and complicated. And when you finish your first draft, like your nonfiction writing colleagues, you will need to edit, edit, edit. . .

"Don't write merely to be understood. Write so that you cannot possibly be misunderstood." - Robert Louis Stevenson.

10

REVISE AND EDIT, edit,edit...

REVISING AND EDITING your manuscript involves refining, adding, rearranging and cutting material as well as checking punctuation and spelling. Revising is a kind of do-it-yourself content editing. Some writers say drafting a book consists of 10 percent writing and 90 percent rewriting.

You will have to complete at least four drafts to make sure that your work is as thorough, concise, correct and readable as you can make it. These drafts are labeled as follows:

- **First draft** - the rough draft
- **Second draft(s)** - the content edit
- **Third draft** - the peer review
- **Fourth draft** - the copy edit

Before you begin a new draft, put the manuscript aside for awhile. Now might be the time to plan a short vacation. The closer you are to your material the less likely you are to be objective or catch mistakes.

"If at first you don't succeed, you are running about average."
- M. H. Anderson

Second draft: content edit. Perform this step yourself. It is not uncommon for this edit to take as much effort as writing the original manuscript. You must be extremely critical at this point, so take your time.

Look for places in the manuscript that need more information or more attention. Review all your original research material to make sure nothing has been left out. Do any further research necessary to fill the holes that appear. Delete the parts that are irrelevant to your purpose. Keep the theme and goal of your book in mind and do not stray from them. Clean up what you have written.

Do not try to do all the rewriting at one time. Carry your manuscript with you in a binder and do what you can when you can. Editing can be fun and it is far easier than the original writing. You have the rough draft on paper, now all you have to do is refine it. Skip around and work on whatever section interests you. Whenever you get a good idea, write it down and put it in the appropriate place in your three ring binder.

Whenever you lose momentum, type up a page with a lot of hand-written notes. This clean-up work has a stimulating effect.

It may take several drafts to polish your work. So what is defined as the second draft could amount to a number of iterations (this book went through eight second drafts).

> *"I can't understand how anyone can write without rewriting everything over and over again. I scarcely ever re-read my published writings, but if by chance I come across a page, it always strikes me: All this must be rewritten; this is how I should have written it."* - Tolstoy.

SECOND DRAFT EVALUATION

You have completed the second draft editing stage when you can answer "yes" to all the following questions:

(   ) **1.** Does my manuscript have all the information needed to give the reader a clear understanding of the subject?

(   ) **2.** Is the information included the most current?

(   ) **3.** Is the manuscript easy to understand and easy to read?

(   ) **4.** Is the order of the material logical and not redundant?

(   ) **5.** Is my manuscript targeted to the market I defined when beginning my book?

If you are writing a work of fiction ask yourself these questions as well.

(   ) **1.** Are the times and locations of my story always clear?

(   ) **2.** Are my characters memorable and do they have distinct personalities?

(   ) **3.** Have any of my characters been lost in the manuscript? Will the reader have trouble tracking them?

(   ) **4.** Is there a strong conflict that continues to build interest?

(   ) **5.** Is my theme clear without being preachy?

(   ) **6.** Does the story entertain?

REFERENCE BOOKS   Some of the reference books you will need at this point are:

- A stylebook such as the *U.S. Government Printing Office Style Manual* or the *Associated Press Stylebook*

- A dictionary (And if you are dealing with a specialized subject get a dictionary on that subject.)

- A book on grammar, punctuation and style such as *Write Right!*

- A thesaurus or dictionary of synonyms and antonyms

- A book on usage such as Fowler's *Modern English Usage* or Bernstein's *The Careful Writer: A Modern Guide to English Usage*

Third draft: peer review. Once you have your manuscript as complete and correct in content as you feel it needs to be, it is time to send it out to other experts in your field to review for technical proofing.

Begin by making a list of everyone you know who might provide valuable input for your manuscript. You may want some of these people to review the entire manuscript while others may only have information on one area or chapter.

Once you have received commitments to review the draft, make a photocopy and ask the experts to make notes right on the copy. Enclose a self-addressed, stamped envelope and remember to give them credit in the acknowledgments. With the peer review, you will not only produce the very best book that you can, you will gain support from "opinion molders" and this is very important to your marketing efforts.

Incidentally, it is customary to pay an honorarium of $50-150 to experts reviewing a book-length manuscript. A peer review is worth much more to you. Many people will not charge for looking over a section or a chapter but it is unfair to expect someone to read an entire manuscript gratis.

A review of your book by three or four people in your field will help find any major problems while providing you with the knowledge that your work is complete. Your peer review will reveal whether your information is correct and if you have left anything out.

The peer review is important even if you are writing fiction. There may be situations or settings based on historical fact or technical processes. Have someone with an extensive background in that area review that part of your manuscript. And it is always desirable to have another writer critique your style.

Incorporate the experts' ideas in the third draft. Retype the manuscript using those comments. Weigh each suggestion. An expert may have a valid point or he or she may have misunderstood what you were trying to convey. In either case, a change is in order.

ASK FRIENDS TO PROOFREAD your manuscript for grammar, punctuation, readability, clarity and content. Have them pencil their comments right on the pages. Do they find the book easy to read? Do they understand what you are saying? If they do not have time to read the whole book, ask them to go over an interesting chapter.

Be careful who you pick. You want someone sympathetic to your project but also someone who can be objective. Do not select someone opposed to your point of view. For example, do not ask a fly fisherman to review your book on bait fishing.

Evaluate every suggestion and decide if or how you wish to incorporate it. Do not feel obligated to make every change.

Fourth draft: copy edit. Edit for copy flow and punctuation. While you probably skipped around from chapter to chapter in the first, second and third drafts, start this editing from

---

"The most valuable of all talents is that of never using two words when one will do." - Thomas Jefferson

the beginning. Go through the manuscript one section at a time and concentrate on grammar, spelling, and punctuation. Try to edit the whole book in just a few days in order to keep the entire manuscript in mind. This makes it easier to spot redundancies or holes in your coverage.

If you are selling your manuscript to a traditional publishing house, it will complete the copy editing. Publishers have "sponsoring editors" who read manuscripts, recommend their purchase and follow them through to production as well as "copy editors" who polish manuscripts. In small houses, the sponsoring and copy editor may be the same person.

11

THE END IS IN SIGHT
Finishing the Manuscript

WHEN TO FINISH If the book is 100 percent accurate and 99 percent complete, go to press. That one last photo and that one extra item can wait for the revised edition. Waiting for one more piece can go on forever. If you delay the publishing, you may miss the market.

THE PROPER LENGTH OF A MANUSCRIPT is precisely what you need to cover the topic completely without being wordy or redundant. Many people feel 60,000 words is a minimum and 100,000 might be a maximum. But some books are very long.

Nonfiction books are not just words. They may have illustrations, tables, resources, blank pages, or other supplementary material. So it is better to think in terms of page count. A book of from 130 to 200 pages is desirable. Make sure the book has enough "heft" to be considered a book but not so many pages that it becomes expensive to produce and threatening to the reader.

THE FINISHED MANUSCRIPT must be typed, never handwritten. The manuscript should be neatly double-spaced on one side of 8½ x 11 white paper and contain a minimum number of changes. If your work is in a word processor, you can easily print a clean new edition of the manuscript. If you lack either the ability or desire to type the final draft, there are many typists who specialize in this work. Check with business schools and look for secretarial services in the Yellow Pages. Typists' rates are moderate.

START EACH CHAPTER about one-third of the way from the top of the page and make it appear just as you want it in the book by listing the chapter number and title. At the top of each page, type your name and the chapter/page number. Leave about a one inch margin all around the page so you and the typesetter will have room for penciling in notes. If you maintain consistency in line length and in lines per page, it will be easier to project the length of the finished book. If you type the final draft yourself, you will have an opportunity to clean it up and make the text flow even better.

PROOFREADER'S MARKS are standardized to enable you to communicate clearly with your editor, typesetter and printer. A complete set of marks can be found in your dictionary under "proofreader's marks." Stick to the standard marks. If you make up your own, you will only confuse those who must understand them. Use these marks throughout the editing/proofreading process.

PROOFREADER'S MARKS

ℒ or ℐ or ⁊   delete; take it out

⌒   close up; print as one word

ℬ   delete and close up

∧ or > or ⋏   caret; insert here ⎧something

insert a space

eℰ#   space evenly where indicated

stet   let marked text stand as set

tr   transpose; change order the

/ used to separate two or more marks and often as a concluding stroke at the end of an insertion

---

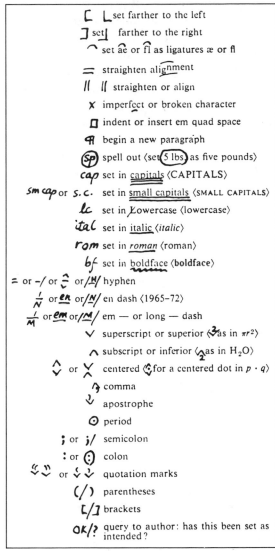

⎡ ⎣set farther to the left

⎤ set⏋ farther to the right

⌒ set a͡e or f͡l as ligatures æ or fl

⹀ straighten align͡ment

∥ ‖ straighten or align

✗ imperf̧ect or broken character

▯ indent or insert em quad space

¶ begin a new paragraph

(SP) spell out ⟨set 5 lbs. as five pounds⟩

cap set in capitals ⟨CAPITALS⟩

sm cap or *s.c.* set in small capitals ⟨SMALL CAPITALS⟩

lc set in /lowercase ⟨lowercase⟩

ital set in italic ⟨*italic*⟩

rom set in roman ⟨roman⟩

bf set in boldface ⟨**boldface**⟩

= or –/ or ⌒ or /ᴴ/ hyphen

$\frac{1}{N}$ or *en* or /N/ en dash ⟨1965–72⟩

$\frac{1}{M}$ or *em* or /M/ em — or long — dash

∨ superscript or superior ⟨²as in πr^2⟩

∧ subscript or inferior ⟨₂as in H_2O⟩

⌃⌄ or ⋎ centered ⟨⁀for a centered dot in $p \cdot q$⟩

⌢ comma

ᵛ apostrophe

⊙ period

; or ;/ semicolon

: or ⊙ colon

⹂ ⹂ or ⌄ ⌄ quotation marks

(/) parentheses

[/] brackets

OK/? query to author: has this been set as intended?

ARTWORK   Illustrations consist of line work and halftones. Line work is a clean black on white drawing without any shading. Line drawings may be pasted directly on the boards unless their size must be enlarged or reduced. Halftones are made from photographs, or drawings with shading, by taking a photograph of them through a screen. You will notice the result by looking at a printed photograph through a magnifying glass. A screened photograph is composed of many tiny dots of various sizes (shading).

If you need line work and cannot draw, you can hire a commercial artist. Most typesetters have illustrators on their staff or know some. These artists usually work inexpensively. See the collaboration chapter for a discussion of hiring and paying illustrators.

Your typesetter or printer may also have a large file of "clip art" and you may find something there you can use. Clip art books are commercially-provided drawings on a large variety of subjects that may be used without further copyright permission. However, most clip art seems dated. Many people lift art from reprints of old Sears catalogs and other publications where the copyright has expired. Depending on your subject, you may find useful drawings in certain military and government publications which are in the public domain.

PHOTOS AND DRAWINGS are easily indicated in the manuscript with page and position numbers. The second photo on page 40 of Chapter Three would be marked "3-40-B", for example. Mark the location both in the manuscript and on the back of the photo or drawing. Mark the photo near its edge and do not press too hard, you may push through to damage the photo. Incidentally, it is sometimes necessary to indicate which side of the photo goes up if it is not obvious to someone unfamiliar with the subject. Type the captions into the manuscript under the photo position number. Make photocopies of the photos or contact prints and paste them into the manuscript (set the copy machine on "light"). This will make the manuscript clearer to both you and those who edit or proof for you. Never paste in the photos themselves; they are hard to get off and may be damaged.

PHOTOGRAPHS, rarely seen in fiction, are almost a requirement in nonfiction, especially in how-to books. The most successful how-to books are those that integrate words and pictures to form an attractive teaching tool. Unless you are writing an art-type book, you will use black and white rather than the more expensive color. Color requires four trips through the press plus pre-press "color separations." The best photos are large, (they become sharper when reduced) glossy, black and whites with a lot of contrast. Color photos and slides may be reproduced in black and white but they usually appear somewhat muddy. Photographs which have already been printed once may be pasted-in directly or reduced and res-creened, but the results are not as good as with an original glossy photo. When in doubt about the suitability of a photo, ask a printer. Occasionally the screening actually improves the photo.

USING THE CAMERA　As you compile your manuscript, make a photo list so you will know what pictures you need. Then set out with your gear to take them. Try to include only the object, person or activity you are trying to show; avoid distracting clutter. For good black and white contrast, avoid tonal shades.

Put people in your photos. If you are showing a number of pieces of clothing which are better modeled, invite as many different people as possible to wear them. You can bet that each model will buy a copy of the book. When taking still shots of people, make them smile. Get their teeth in the picture. Most people do not know how to pose for a photo and complain that they do not photograph well. Catch them smiling and they will love you for it. Try to capture action in your photos, make them move. Seek the unusual, tell a story, look for human interest, shoot from a different angle.

Then have your film processed by a custom photo lab. Do not send it out through your supermarket. Slides do not matter as much but in black and white processing the enlarger must be carefully and precisely focused.

Photographs slated for screening and printed reproduc-tion should have more contrast. Tell the photo processor that the photos are "for reproduction." The resulting photo-graphic prints will appear slightly harsh.

Handle negatives and photos carefully, you have a lot invested in them. Keep them clean and mail them flat between cardboard sheets.

When you want the typesetter or printer to crop a print, do not take out the scissors; make crop marks on the edges of the photographic print. If a photo needs retouching (to remove an extraneous object like your camera bag, for example), let the graphic artist do it. Do not use paper clips. For more information on cameras and photography, see the discussion in *Writer's Market*.

Photo release forms are advisable, particularly for pictures of minors. Permission might cost $20-500 but normally your subjects are just tickled to be in the book. A news photo does not require a release unless it is used in an advertisement. A release form may consist of a simple statement giving permission to use a photo in return for a stated amount of money.

OTHER PHOTO SOURCES Freelancers with a stock of photos will sell them in quantity for a couple of dollars each. Or you can have them custom shot for $5-$20 per photo. When dealing with professional photographers, get prices in advance. Prices will vary greatly with experience. The chamber of commerce, private firms, trade associations and some governmental departments have public relations departments who provide photos as part of their function. Libraries and museums sometimes have photo files but museums often charge for the photographs and restrict you to a one-time use. If you publish a second printing, they get another use fee.

Photo syndicates are in the business of selling stock photos. Some are The Image Bank (8228 Sunset #310, 90046) in Los Angeles and the Bettmann Archive (136 East 57th), Underwood & Underwood (3 West 46th St.) and Comstock (32 East 31 Street, 10016) in New York. Syndicates belonging to the American Society of Magazine Publishers charge royalties of about $125.00 for one-time use of a half-page black and white photo.

The Library of Congress has a vast collection of historical photographs and will make prints for you if they have the negative. For a catalog, write to the Library of Congress, Prints and Photographs Division, Washington, DC 20540. Also see the National Archives (Ninth & Constitution) and the Smithsonian Institution, in Washington D.C. Picture sources are listed in *World Photography Sources* by Bradshaw, *Writer's Market and Literary Market Place*.

Photos from old books with expired copyrights are easily copied with your camera. Just carry the book over to the light, lay it out flat and snap a photo. These photos of photos come out very nicely.

When covering an event, make contact with the other photographers and get their business cards. They may have just what you need.

MAILING THE MANUSCRIPT The big day has arrived. You will either be sending your manuscript off to your publisher or, if self-publishing, off to your typesetter. If your publisher or typesetter is not nearby, you will have to ship the manuscript. Stack the photos and drawings and enclose them in cardboard to avoid folding. Send the manuscript in a binder. Enclose both in plastic bags and pack them in a sturdy cardboard carton. The Post Office does offer a special manuscript rate (same as book rate) but most authors prefer United Parcel Service because the service is good and the parcel must be signed for on the receiving end. If you are not near a UPS office, you might use certified, priority (air) mail through the Post Office. A couple of extra dollars now is well worth the expense. Be sure the carton contains your complete return address.

Always keep a copy of the manuscript. This is to protect you in case the original is lost in the mail or by the printer. And it is your ready reference when the publisher or typesetter calls with questions. Take the manuscript to a copy center. They usually give reduced rates for overnight service and are reasonably inexpensive. After the book is printed, turn the copies over; the paper makes a fine scratch pad and people love to get notes on it.

Writing a book is a manageable project if you have a system. With the organization outlined here, your decision to go, and a little discipline, you can start a whole new rewarding life.

"It is hard to be good at what you do—even harder to be great. But when the job is finished and the results are better than anyone expected, there's a feeling of pride that wells up inside you and makes it all worthwhile."

12

HOW DO YOU AUTHOR A BOOK WHEN YOU CAN'T WRITE?

There is a difference between being an *author* and being a *writer*. An author creates material, while a writer commits material to paper. There are many authors with a lifetime of experience and there are many very good writers who do not have the experience or expertise required to write a book-length manuscript. The solution is to introduce these two types of people. By combining the knowledge of the expert/creator with the talent and training of the professional writer the odds of producing a superior product are very favorable. Some people cannot write because they:

- Do not have enough time
- Do not like to write
- Consider themselves idea people
- Do not have the patience
- Do not have the training to be polished writers
- Cannot make the emotional commitment to this type of solitude and perseverence

If you cannot afford to take time from your career to become an expert writer, it may be more practical and cost effective to leave the writing of the manuscript to a writing professional. If, for example, your "other" work pays you $50 to $100 per hour, it does not make economic sense to spend time doing work you can buy for $10 or $15 per hour. You may decide to hire a typist, editor, co-author, ghostwriter or other collaborator.

au'thŏr, *n.* [ME. *autour*; OFr. *autor*; L. *auctor*, author, from *augere*, to cause to grow, increase.]
1. one who produces, creates, or brings into being; the beginner, creator, or first mover of anything.
2. one who composes or writes a book, or whose occupation is to compose and write books.
writ'ēr, *n.* 1. one who writes, has written, or is in the habit of writing.
2. a person whose business or occupation is writing; specifically, (a) a copyist; a scribe or clerk; (b) an author, journalist, or the like.

With permission. From *Webster's New Twentieth Century Dictionary*, Second Edition. Copyright © 1983 by Simon & Schuster, Inc.

TEAM APPROACH Behind most authors is a small army of support troops. They may be content editors, copy editors, technical editors, readers, researchers, indexers, proofreaders, literary scouts, agents, librarians, publisher's representatives, translators or anyone else who offers a service connected with book writing. You have to decide what kind of help you need and what you can afford. To help you, we will relate some actual partnership stories.

Jim Comiskey is a successful businessman who does not type. When he decided to author a book, he took a strictly business approach and paid for the help he needed. He read up on his subject, conducted interviews, researched the topic and made an outline. Then he hand-wrote the first draft. After reviewing and editing his writing, he dictated the manuscript for How to Start, Expand & Sell a Business *into a tape recorder and sent it to a word processing service. He located the service through a local university by asking for a "thesis typist with word processing equipment." His slow speech allowed the typists to type straight off the tape recorder; they did not even need a dictating machine with foot pedal.*

Jim edited the hard copy printout and gave it back to the service for entering. The cost was $15 per hour and, even with many revisions, amounted to only $1,800. Then he sent a clean version to a professional editor to check punctuation and grammar. This editor was found through a local writers' group and the thorough editing cost $1,000.

Once again, the manuscript was returned to the word processing service to enter the corrections. The floppy disk was sent to a typesetter to avoid more keystroking and proofing. The typesetter charged $1,500 to set the type and to pasteup the 8½ x 11, 265 page book.

Jim paid $1,000 for the cover art. He found the artist through a listing in Literary Market Place. *Because he dictated his book, Jim did not have to learn to type or improve his handwriting. Because he relied on professional editors, he did not have to learn punctuation or grammar. The result is an original book in a conversational style. It is receiving excellent reviews.*

DICTATING If you cannot type, try dictation. If you can speak in a logical, informative fashion, you can dictate for transcribing; get a tape recorder. Do the transcriptions yourself or hire a secretary. Then edit the hard copy and either correct the language or leave it as is. Sometimes a basic speaking style adds to the book.

When dictating, you need an outline and notes if you want the manuscript to flow in any sort of order. Dictation will help you get your message on paper, but you still need to be organized.

Barbara Cartland, the queen of romantic novels (350 million copies of her books are in print), dictates her novels to a secretary. So far she has authored more than 200 books this way. One year, working between 1:00 p.m. and 3:30 p.m., she talked out twenty-two books at the rate of 6-7,000 words (one chapter) per day. Now 83, she still "writes" up to 30,000 words a week. Cartland dreams up a plot, follows the romance formula and then lets the story flow in her famous story-telling style.

WHEN YOU DON'T HAVE THE TIME TO WRITE Many people today have tremendous ideas, a great store of infor-mation, and creative approaches. But they are so busy they do not have time to write a book. These people need collaborators.

Mindy Bingham is an organizer, an idea-person and a doer whose creative mind never shuts off but she moves too fast to polish her writing and she does not dwell on proper spell-ing. Mindy took the Girls Club of Santa Barbara in financial crisis, turned it around and made the service organization a financial success by authoring and producing a book on the Club's behalf. She envisioned a book for teenage girls on self-awareness and personal planning. She roughed it out incorporating the exercises and questionnaires she had devel-oped, had Judy Edmondson research and write other parts and then shipped the whole manuscript off to Sandy Stryker in Los Angeles. Sandy, a former newspaper reporter and now an advertising copy writer, rewrote the book contrib-uting flow, continuity, style and zip. The book, recognized as a classic in its field, would never have come about if these three women with diverse talents had not come together as a team.

COLLABORATION is often the marriage of an expert/author who does not have the time or ability to write and a writer without original material. Or, it may be a co-authorship of experts in like or dissimilar fields. Which of the following types of collaboration would work best for you?

> *"I love being a writer. What I can't stand is the paperwork."* - Peter DeVries.

CO-AUTHORSHIP involves two or more people. Often all participants are recognized experts. Ideally, they are also equally competent writers, but this is a rare occurrence, indeed. They may contribute equally to the workload, or one partner may carry a heavier burden. Probably the person with the most recognized name will do less of the actual writing, but more of the content editing.

Gordon Burgett is an author/publisher who spends a good part of the year traveling the California state college circuit teaching classes on writing, publishing, speaking, cassette tape publishing and how to give seminars. Mike Frank is a well-known professional speaker. Gordon's writing is technically excellent and he is a great speaker but Mike is better known in speaking circles. The two joined together to produce the manuscript for Speaking For Money. *Each wrote in his area of expertise and then Burgett did the rewriting, editing and publishing.*

Dan Poynter shared the responsibilities for the Frisbee Players' Handbook *with disc champion Mark Danna. Danna wrote the throwing and catching chapters while Poynter wrote on history, record attempts, competition and also assembled the appendix. While Poynter came up with the unique package and marketing idea, he did not have enough expertise or credibility as a Frisbee player to produce a book that would be taken seriously. Mark Danna rounded out the team well.*

If you have a book you want to do yourself but recognize that you lack the required technical expertise, consider co-authorship. Find an expert in the field to write the technical part while you write the other part and then each of you can edit the other's material. This approach has many advantages including the endorsement of an expert, credibility and someone else to send on the promotional tour. The disadvantages are smaller royalties, extra accounting and author handholding.

A doctor, who is also an excellent writer (and who asked his name not be used), collaborated with another doctor who was a nationally recognized expert in a new surgical technique. The writer doctor did most of the actual work while the doctor with the name in the field did final editing and lent his name to the work. Though the workload was unequal, the doctors shared the royalties equally. And, as a result of the book, the writer doctor made a name for himself in a new and exciting field.

THE EXPERT/WRITER TEAM can be successful even if the writer joins the project knowing nothing about the proposed subject. It is the expert's responsibility to provide the research, data, and experience that will make the book valuable. When two people collaborate in this manner, it may seem that the writer is doing more work because he or she is spending more time on the project than the expert. The writer must remember that a lot of the expert's work was done long before the writer came into the project. The expert has spent years perfecting and increasing his or her knowledge. Be sure to discuss who will do what and how much at the beginning of the collaboration process to avoid hard feelings later on. Use the responsibility chart in Chapter Thirteen to clarify roles.

SPOUSES AS WRITING PARTNERS   The first place to look for a writing partner is your spouse. Maybe you have one of those relationships where opposites attract. One of you is detail/research-oriented while the other has a creative mind that never shuts off. If at least one of you is a competent writer, why not team up on your book?

Sit down together and go over the four T's in Chapter Two. If between the two of you, you can answer most of the questions in the affirmative, you have the makings of a great writing partnership.

> "Writing is no trouble: you just jot down ideas as they occur to you. The jotting is simplicity itself—it is the occurring which is difficult." - Stephen Leacock

Teresa and Raf Dahlquist teamed up for a series of books. Together, they developed a charming line of whimsically illustrated children's stories about famous scientists. Their first was Mr. Halley and His Comet. *Raf is a highly technical scientist who does the research while Teresa is the idea-person who writes the prose.*

Even if one spouse has no experience outside the home, a project like this gets both of them published, provides them with a common project (which may do great things for the marriage) and elevates their job status.

WRITING BY COMMITTEE Many textbooks are written by committee. If two heads are better than one does it hold true that three, four or five are better still? It can be. But, as the number of authors moves from two to three or more, it becomes more difficult to keep the manuscript tight, the communication clear and the workloads equal while still allowing some creativity to filter in. The committee members must remember that they are a team. They must work up a game plan that will outline everyone's responsibilities clearly, diagram the decision-making process and provide deadlines. In Chapter Thirteen you will find responsibility and decision-making charts that can help clarify responsibilities, avoid conflict, and eliminate duplication of effort.

GHOSTWRITERS write for money not for fame—their name does not go on the cover of the book. How many ghostwriters do you know? Would you know one if you saw one? Ghost writers, by definition, are invisible. They write your book for you from your notes and thoughts.

These writers usually deal in autobiography. Most celebrity books are ghosted. Ghosts often obtain information through interviews (both the "author" and everyone around him or her) and then flesh out the material and commit it to paper. This interviewing may take quite a bit of time because the ghost has to get to know the author well. The drafts are returned to the "author" for content editing and are then rewritten by the invisible collaborator.

Ghostwriting a book can take as much as two years so it can be costly. If you are famous, ghosts will often write for fifty percent of the advance and royalties because they know the book will be published by a major publisher. If you are not famous, you will normally pay the ghost a flat fee. Those who get a percentage may do a better job as they care more about the success of the book. This kind of collaboration costs more than editing or co-authoring because ghosts do a greater amount of the work.

Ghosts should get some credit in the book. He or she may be mentioned in the acknowledgments or the copyright page may contain a statement such as "Packaged and produced by Sheri Simmen."

Poets and fiction writers sometimes turn to ghosting to buy time for their own work. Many find it to be good practice.

CONTRACT WRITING requires even less "author" input than ghosting. Often the author provides only the subject, some unique ideas and an indication of the direction the project should follow. Contracted books are often wrapped up in less than sixty days by moonlighting advertising copywriters or journalists. Many nonfiction books, other than autobiographies, are contracted. These books might be company histories, manuals for a new product, or how-to books.

Joe Karbo was famous for his Lazy Man's Way to Riches. *His full-page ads featuring small type and large hype started a new trend in advertising copywriting. Even after he passed away a few years ago, the small book continued to sell at $10 a copy—for a total of over nine million dollars so far. The untold story is that Joe paid to have his idea written. His investment was less than $3,000.*

"*The man of science appears to be the only man who has something to say just now—and the only man who does not know how to say it."* - Sir James Barrie.

Many of the more successful book houses approach publishing from a hard-nosed marketing position. They know what they have been able to sell in the past and they stay in their field of expertise often by assigning writers to produce more of these "contracted books." Magazine editors have always relied on freelancers, so buying the material from others is not new or unusual.

Once you have decided on an area of concentration, you too may approach others to write for you by paying cash outright or using modest royalty advances as an inducement. The accounting is easier and the arrangement is often more cost effective if you pay outright for the help you need. Flat fees are often around $2,500 for a short book, half to be paid on assignment and half on acceptance. Contracted writers should be paid on a schedule. They usually do not share in the copyright, and generally do not receive editorial control over the work. The writer sells his or her labor and has no further claim to it.

EDITORS Perhaps you can get your thoughts down on paper but all that good information does not read very well. What you need is an editor, someone who can take your information and clean it up.

Editors may be the basic copy editors who dot "i's" and cross "t's" or they may be rewrite editors who add zip to your writing: energy, order and clarity.

A professional editing job can make a major difference in manuscript success and acceptability. If you do not have a strong journalistic background, editors are a good investment.

> *"There is nothing wrong with writing poorly but there is no excuse for not having it cleaned up by an editor."*

"Lost time is never found again" - Benjamin Franklin

13

FINDING AND WORKING WITH A WRITING PARTNER

If you have decided not to go it alone, here are some ideas for finding and working with a collaborator.

WHAT TYPE OF PARTNER DO YOU NEED? Do you need a little light proofreading help? Does your work require major editing? Do you want someone you can work with to get your message down on paper in readable form? Re-evaluate your strengths and limitations by reviewing your Author Workplan chart in Chapter Two. Do you need a co-author, ghost writer, contract writer, editor, researcher, or typist?

If your book is nonfiction, you want a nonfiction writer, not a poet. The applicant should have a track record; do not hire a novice. Look for someone with experience in writing books, not just short magazine articles.

Draft a job description, establish a work timetable and make up a rough contract. Clarify in your own mind what type of help you want and what you want to have done. Prepare for the interview by having a job description, work schedule and contract written up.

DRAFTING THE JOB DESCRIPTION   Your job description should include the following:

1. Job title
2. Working title of the book

3. Required qualifications for the position

4. What examples of the applicant's work you would like to see

5. A draft of your work timetable

6. How the writer will be credited in the book

7. Duties of the applicant, if hired

8. Salary or remuneration schedule

SAMPLE JOB DESCRIPTION

1. **Job title:** Contract writer.

2. **Title of work:** *The Cat and Dog Handbook.*

3. **Qualifications:** Experienced in the field of nonfiction writing. The ability to research, outline, draft and write an approximately 150-page, 5½ x 8½-book in the area of dog and cat care.

4. **Portfolio** review required. Samples of past work.

5. **Schedule:**
   Contract writer completes research—1/1/86.
   Contract writer completes first draft of book—3/1/86.
   Author completes content edit—3/31/86.
   Contract writer completes second draft—4/30/86.
   Author sends out for peer review to be completed by—6/30/86.
   Contract writer completes third draft—7/15/86.
   Contract writer completes final copy edit and manuscript by 7/30/86.

6. **Contract writer** shall receive co-author status with Author.

7. **Contract writer** shall be responsible for all research, writing and editing of the manuscript. The work will be completed when it is in correct form to be delivered to the typesetter. Contracting Author shall be responsible for providing necessary research direction, content editing of the first draft and locating the peer reviewers for the third draft.

8. **Compensation** shall be paid at the rate of _____. (See discussion.)

WHERE TO FIND A WRITING PARTNER Start by looking in the Yellow Pages under "Writers," "Editorial Services," and "Secretarial Services"; try this one right now. Notice how easy it is to find help. Check *Literary Market Place* under "Editorial Services." Here you will find a number of agencies and individuals offering a wide variety of collaborative help.

Typical ads (addresses deleted)

Publishers Weekly, Small Press and *Writer's Digest* have classified sections with ads from collaborators. Those who advertise tend to be more professional.

Contact local writers' groups, editorial services and secretarial services through local bookstores and libraries. They know the people in the writing profession in your locale. Be a detective and follow each lead.

To contact people in the "word game," go to PR firms, or advertising agencies, and see the *Writer's Digest Yearbook*. *Freelancers of North America* lists editors, ghostwriters, collaborators, and technical writers. You should find a number of names here.

If you need research assistance, look for a librarian who wants some moonlighting work. Also try the local college where you will find students happy to work at minimum wage. The lucky student may even be able to obtain college credit while working with you. Credit in your acknowledgements may help them later in their career search and it also looks good on their resume. Check the telephone directory and call the student placement office. Of course, you could place your own help-wanted ad.

GHOST WRITER for self-help manuscripts. Living money, royalties. Executive Reno home. Travel. Prefer female to age 45.

Wanted: Experienced writer. Expand corporate intrigue and dialogue. Condensed novel. Material recognized world wide. Potential block buster. Will split %. Resume.

Pro Ghost. Need Ludlum style writer to complete manuscript. Outline plus 100 pages finished. Top talent a must. Resume, etc.

WANTED: Writer, living in KC area, to work with author on nonfiction book. Write Will

Example of short ads for a ghostwriter

Look for newspaper reporters with some extra time. They are professionals who are used to deadlines. Reporters are trained to listen and to put your thoughts down accurately. Once they have your material written out, you may edit the work. Reporters are also used to having their material edited and do not have too much of their ego tied up in it. The reporter may even wind up doing a feature story on you— And their media contacts are invaluable.

> *Donald Dible, author/publisher of* Up Your Own Organization, *says, "Avoid grade school and high school English teachers. For the most part, they are more concerned with discovering what is wrong with your writing (remember the red ink on your themes?) than in helping you fix it for publication."*

Word of mouth is often the best method for finding help, especially when searching locally. One freelancer will often lead you to others. Writing clubs and other trade associations will usually pass on names, and since they are concerned about their own credibility, you can be reasonably certain the people they recommend will be competent. You should be able to come up with the partner you need. The result should be help for you, work for your partner, and a much better book for your readers.

WHAT TO LOOK FOR IN A PARTNER

- **Compatibility** You must not only get along and work easily with your temporary partner, you must like each other. You will be working very closely in this temporary marriage; you are handing over a segment of your life to this person.

  Make sure the chemistry is right. Does your writer grasp your aims and goals quickly? You should be able to work together so that the result is greater than the sum of the individual contributions. Your partner may do some things better than you—that is what a good partnership is all about. Is there mutual trust? Some people are very protective about what they commit to paper and editing their work can cause unnecessary strain in the working relationship. Be sure to cover this topic thoroughly in the interview before agreeing to hire the writer.

- **Quality of work.** Your collaborator should have experience in nonfiction book writing if the book is nonfiction or in fiction writing if the book is fiction. Be wary of the person who has never written as a professional. This includes well-meaning instructors of English or journalism as well as the casual journal or magazine writer. Writing is a craft, a profession that requires practice and persistence. If your partner does not approach writing in a business-like way, you may have problems. You do not need a collaborator who is egocentric, undiplomatic or unreliable.

- **Quantity of work.** If you are hiring an editor, does he or she dot "i's," correct grammar and spelling or do you need a complete rewrite? Evaluate your own writing ability and hire the kind of editor you need. There is a big difference in areas of expertise.

  Doctor Hartbrodt wrote a medical book about a common disease. The manuscript contained a lot of solid, helpful information but was hard to read. He contacted writers' groups, editorial services and secretarial services through the Yellow Pages and located four people who were willing to help. He gave each a copy of the first chapter and asked them to edit a couple of sample pages and to quote their fee. Some editors only want to dot "i's" and cross "t's" while others want to do complete rewrites. Using this method, he was able to compare their work and select the one he liked at the best per-page price.

"Be very cautious about partnerships. They seem to be so easy to get into and so difficult to get out of." - Jim Comiskey in *How to Start, Expand & Sell a Business.*

- **Compatible work styles.** You and your partner must have the same level of commitment. If one partner is hard-working and can work on past quitting time to get something done right while the other would rather watch the sunset for inspiration, the union is not likely to last.

- **Price.** Fortunately, the supply of writing help is much greater than the demand. Generally, professionals will cost more. You may get a lower price from someone who is not writing full-time. The best advice is to keep interviewing until you find someone you feel comfortable with who is willing to work at a price you can afford.

INTERVIEW QUESTIONS AND PROCESS Make your first cut over the telephone. Do not waste your time or theirs if there is a reason they should not work for you. Tell callers about your project, your schedule, the proposed length of the manuscript, and so on. In addition, ask them about any specific requirements you might have unrelated to the project. Keep a list of questions by the telephone. They might include:

- What is your experience in writing? (or editing, typing, etc.).
- Do you have experience in the subject?
- Can you meet the time schedule?
- Do you have a car?
- Are you allergic to cats?
- Do you smoke?

If you have a cat, don't want someone smoking in your home and are far from public transportation, save time and take care of these questions now.

Mail a copy of your job description to the candidates who pass the initial telephone interview. Use a cover letter to ask them to review the job description and invite them to set up an interview by a given date. This process will save you some time. If your job description is clearly written and complete, the applicant will understand exactly what you want and can make the decision to proceed.

At the interview, have a draft copy of your contract and timetable ready to share with people you think may be finalists. Explain that it is a draft and that some points may be negotiable. When you make your final choice, go over the contract and job description carefully so that all changes can be put in writing before the final agreement is reached.

These potential partners should provide a list of their services, clients they have worked for (references), a resume and samples of their work. Do not expect a lot of free consulting though applicants may have some off- the-cuff ideas. Listen to their questions as the best indication of their basic approach, thoroughness and understanding of your situation. Be wary if they betray the confidence of other clients. If they tell on others, they will tell on you.

Follow up on references for finalists. These references should be from people they have worked for in the past in the capacity that you are considering hiring them. Repeat business is the sign of a successful professional writer.

Be sure to check on the following traits when you call references:

1. The ability to take editorial direction
2. The ability to meet deadlines
3. The ability to follow-through until completion
4. The quality of their work
5. The candidate's strong points
6. The candidate's weak points

"The closest to perfection a person ever comes is when he fills out a job application form." - Stanley J. Randall

Look for a writer who is businesslike. One who shows up on time with samples and resumes and seems to know what he or she is doing.

When hiring an editor, ask each applicant to edit the same sample two to three pages and to submit a per-page quote. If you don't know the work style of the editor, paying by the hour can be dangerously expensive and you will not want to be standing over anyone with a whip.

A professional will find out your requirements and goals and will help direct your interview session. At the end of the meeting ask the writer to send you a written quote.

Never hire the first interviewee who walks through the door. Interview ten or more and then select the best one.

PARTNERSHIPS THAT HAPPEN. You might be reading this book because the project you have in mind was conceived by two people. In other words, you already have your partner. These writing partners are usually co-workers or friends. The books they produce often begin over a cup of coffee, at a conference or a social affair when you begin to dream together of a book that is "really needed!" It is often hard to make "partnerships that happen" work. So stop right now and complete the author workplan in Chapter Two. Identify your individual strengths and weaknesses and then work up a plan assigning each of you the most appropriate responsibilities. A workplan will make book authoring a much more rewarding and positive experience for you both.

HOW TO TREAT YOUR PARTNER Your collaborator is a professional and must be treated fairly. This means paying your partner as agreed, on time. Do not change the parameters of the project without discussion, renegotiation and reduction to writing. Give all the help, background information, time and materal he or she requires to do a good job for you.

> *"It was a friendship founded on business, which is a good deal better than a business founded on friendship."* - John D. Rockefeller

Decide how you want to trade material back and forth. Will it be chapter by chapter or manuscript by manuscript? The faster each of you work, the greater the amount of material you can trade. You want to be able to keep the work in mind so that when the other partner calls, you will know what he or she is talking about.

Clearly establish responsibilities. Each partner must be responsible for specific tasks and have definite deadlines. Projects with two or more partners sometimes fail because certain tasks were left to the "other" partner. Or the work done is redundant.

Communication is very important in a partnership. Time should be set aside periodically to sit down and talk about what is going on, to address new ideas and to improve the project or process. Partners must feel that they can freely state their concerns and that the genuine goal of each person is to create as good a product as possible.

WRITING BY COMMITTEE is where more than two people are contributing to the manuscript. When working with a group there are some important guidelines:

- One senior author should have final approval power for all manuscript decisions, and this must be understood by all involved before the project begins. The senior author should be someone who can make decisions quickly and comfortably, even when others disagree.

- The final draft of all work must be written by the same person to achieve a smooth flow and continuity of style.

- Explicit timetables and responsibilities must be negotiated, agreed to and adhered to.

"I've always believed in writing without a collaborator, because where two people are writing the same book, each believes he gets all the worries and only half the royalties." - Agatha Christie.

● Regular meetings must be held at predetermined times with written agendas and with commitments for attendance by all involved.

● There must be a termination clause in the contract in case one member decides to leave or is unable to fulfill his or her commitment. A termination clause tells all concerned what the alternative is to completing the project, and sets out the process for removing someone from the work.

RESPONSIBILITY AND DECISION-MAKING CHARTS. On whatever basis you hire help or work with partners, you must agree in advance on how you plan to divide the work. Each of you must know and understand the limits and obligations the agreement imposes on you both. One way is to develop an outline and then assign responsibility with deadlines to each part of the project. The timetable must be realistic.

Here is a responsiblity chart for two co-authors who are doing a nonfiction book on how to open a boutique. Wendy is the expert/idea person and Nancy is a professional writer who works as a newspaper reporter. Neither of them feels totally competent to do the final copy edit on the book so they have decided to hire a copy editor. This chart provides a clear map showing how and when the tasks will be completed.

The **R** indicates the person responsible for initiating a task and seeing it through to completion.

RESPONSIBILITY CHART FOR BOUTIQUE BOOK (TWO PEOPLE)

Task	Wendy	Nancy	Projected completion date
PREPARATION			
Set up binder	R		1/30/86
Gather all books and magazines	R		2/15/86
Write for information	R		2/1/86
Write outline of book	R		3/1/86
Organize in "pilot system"	R		3/15/86
FIRST DRAFT			
Outline each chapter	R		4/30/86
Complete first draft		R	7/30/86
SECOND DRAFT			
Review for gaps	R		8/86
Research to fill gaps	R		8/30/86
Edit first draft	R		9/15/86
Complete second draft		R	10/15/86
List needed photos and drawings	R		9/30/86
THIRD DRAFT			
Locate peer reviewers	R		10/1/86
Manage manuscript transfers	R		10/15/86
Edit peer notes	R		11/15/86
Rewrite third draft		R	12/1/86
FOURTH DRAFT			
Hire copy editor	R		11/15/86
Enter changes and prepare final manuscript	R		12/30/86

Task	Wendy	Nancy	Projected completion date
MANUSCRIPT FINALIZATION Write for permissions	R		12/30/86
Footnotes		R	12/30/86
Bibliography		R	12/30/86
Appendix		R	12/30/86
Table of contents		R	12/30/86
Send ABI and for LC	R		12/30/86
Final check on statistics		R	12/30/86
See that clean copy is complete		R	1/1/87
Send printed book for copyright	R		

The following decision-making chart outlines the tasks, responsibilities and communication structure for a committee of college professors working on a textbook. Decision making within a group of three or more people can become very cumbersome. What happens is either too much time is spent polling the committee on how members feel a task should be handled or not enough input is received from committee members and they feel their ideas and opinions are not valued. In either case, tension is created and valuable energy and time are diverted. That time and energy should go into manuscript production. Developing a decision-making chart in the beginning will help eliminate frustration later on.

RESPONSIBILITY AND DECISION MAKING CHART
For committee working on a college textbook
for thoroughbred racehorse breeding

Codes:

A = This person has final approval. He or she may veto a project or direction.

R = This person is responsible for initiating a task and seeing it through to completion.

C = This person wants to be consulted before a decision is made on a task but has no veto power.

I = This person needs to be informed on what the final decision is but does not have to be consulted.

Task	Author A	Author B	Author C	Author D	Completion date
Complete chapter order	R	C	C	C	1/30/86
Outline of the book	R	C	C	C	3/1/86
Complete research and draft appropriate chapters in the areas of: Nutrition		R			6/1/86
Veterinary practice		R			7/15/86
Bloodlines	R		C		6/1/86
Farm management	C		R		6/1/86
Stallion management		C		R	6/1/86
Bloodmare care		C		R	7/15/86
Foaling		R		C	9/1/86
Pasture management			C	R	9/1/86
Financial administration	C		R		7/15/86

Task	Author A	Author B	Author C	Author D	Completion date
Personnel	C		R		9/1/86
The future of racing	R				7/15/86
Content editing of total manuscript	R				9/20/86
Locate peer reviewers and facilitate review process		R	R	I	6/1/86
Write for permissions	I		R		10/1/86
Completion of index	I	R			10/1/86
Negotiate contract with publisher	A	C	R	C	6/1/86
Accuracy of footnotes	I		R		10/1/86
Responsible for total rewrite of the manuscript	A			R	10/15/86
Copy editing for spelling and grammar				R	11/15/86
Responsible for producing final clean copy	A			R	12/1/86
Monitor of decision-making chart	A				
Call meetings of authors	R				monthly
Name the book	A	C	C	C	11/1/86
List of and resources for photos	A		R		11/1/86

DECISION MAKING CHART

A sample decision-making chart for a cookbook written by a committee of community volunteers for their favorite charity

Task	Committee chair	Author B	Author C	Author D	Author E	Completion date
Outline the book with chapter headings	A	R	C	C	C	2/1/86
Design recipes, submission form and procedures	A	C	R	C	I	1/15/86
Solicit collaborators and volunteers to submit recipes	R	R	R	R	R	5/1/86
Review, test and edit recipes submitted and research any others in the area of: Hors d'oeuvres, drinks and snacks	A	R				
Main dish and meats	A		R			
Desserts and party section	A			R		
Salads and vegetables	A				R	
Submit draft of each cookbook section	A	R	R	R	R	8/1/86
Rewrite first draft for continuity of style	A			R		10/1/86
Content edit	R	C	C	C	C	11/1/86
Copy edit					R	11/15/86
Prepare final copy of corrected manuscript	A				R	12/1/86
Finalize title	A	C	C	C	C	12/1/86
Decide how to publish the book and conduct necessary negotiations	R	C	C	I	I	12/1/86

A FEW FINAL NOTES ON AUTHORING PARTNERSHIPS.
Teamwork is the key to a good relationship. Avoid the adversary attitude. A good partnership, like a good marriage, can be exciting and very productive. Two people bouncing ideas off one-another can create a much better product.

Each partner must contribute 100 percent to the project every time he or she works on the manuscript. Do not leave rough edges for the other partner to clean up. If you want the example changed, write it, or at least rough it out, yourself. Do not write "change example." "Correcting" or directing the partner does not foster a close working relationship. If you want something in the manuscript, put it in.

It is important to realize there will be certain sentences, sections or editorial comments that are sacred to the other partner. If you are writing back and forth, editing each other's work, and the originator of the material finds a sacred part deleted, changed, or edited, tempers may flare. Establish a communication technique to anticipate this situation. One possibility would be to establish that the word **sacred** used in the margin means that any editing of that part must be done as a joint venture in a formal meeting. Obviously, the word **sacred** should not be used too often or you will bog down the writing and editing process.

When critiquing your partner's work, be sensitive to how you phrase your comments and the approach you take!

> *"No passion in the world is equal to the passion to alter someone else's draft."* - H.G. Wells

COLLABORATORS' 'FAIR FIGHTING' RULES

- Criticize a specific sentence or paragraph, not the other person.

- When discussing a problem area, always finish your observation with..."a better way might be. . ."

- Begin a critique with a positive observation. "What I like is.... What I think needs work is. . . "

- Take turns being the "critic" (devil's advocate).

- Listen to the other person's point of view and be able to restate that view before you react.

- Follow the decision with a wink, smile, hug or kiss (depending on your relationship).

   AND explain to your children (and/or others around you) that you are critically discussing the project, not dis-agreeing with each other.

Collaborative book writing often takes much longer than going it alone. The procedure is slowed because of the joint editing, rewriting and meetings. This is typical committee work. But the trade-off can produce a better product.

"With a good collaborator you find that two heads are, indeed, better than one." - Raymond Hull in *How to Write How-to Books and Articles.*

14

NEGOTIATING AND CONTRACTING
WITH COLLABORATORS

Signing a contract with your collaborator may seem excessively businesslike—as though you do not trust each other. If your collaborator is a close friend or spouse, you may be tempted to skip this chapter altogether. Don't! Written agreements are often more important when people are close.

The object of a writing contract is to clarify thinking and positions of both parties while arriving at a mutually beneficial agreement. You and your collaborator will be working together closely for a long time so both of you have to feel the agreement is consistent and fair.

First-time writers will be eager to become published and may not be terribly concerned about the contract—initially. Many creative people are not business or commercially oriented. It is imperative that contract negotiation and signing be taken care of before the writing begins. Write a rough draft of the contract and ask your potential partner whether it is generally acceptable. Remember that people who write contracts slant them their way. You have an advantage if you draft the contract rather than accept a contract written by the other party. Here is a sample contract with a discussion of some of the items to be considered when an author (you) contracts with a writer.

"A verbal contract isn't worth the paper it's printed on." - Sam Goldwyn, founder of MGM

CONTRACT WRITER WORK AGREEMENT If your collaboration is with a contract writer or ghost, use this contract writer agreement and alter it to fit your situation. This draft will save time by helping you to clarify your own thinking. Then take it to a contract attorney who is familiar with copyright and book publishing. Lawyers work by the hour and **editing** your contract will take less time than starting from scratch.

DRAFT OF A CONTRACT WRITER AGREEMENT

This agreement is made between _____(the Writer) and _____(the Author).

It is agreed that Writer is to write for Author a book approximately _____words in length, provisionally titled _____

It is agreed that the Author will supply all information that the Writer may require to complete the book.

The text and credits are to be framed so as to give the Author full and sole credit as author of the book. Writer agrees to keep the nature of Writer's contribution and the fact that the book will be published under the name of Author, strictly confidential.

If, for the preparation of illustrations for the book, it is necessary to engage artists or photographers, the costs of such work are to be borne entirely by the Author. Otherwise, the entire work and cost of preparing a manuscript fit for publishing, such as research, typing and photocopying, shall be undertaken by the Writer.

Writer is responsibile for securing any copyright clearances.

The responsibility of reading and correcting proofs and compiling an index shall be undertaken by the Writer.

The copyright for the finished work is to be held solely by the Author; all royalties resulting from the sale of the book, or from the sale of subsidiary rights, are to go to the Author

Writer agrees not to use information gained during the preparation of this work to write any competitive work on the same or any allied subject.

Writer acknowledges that all confidential ideas for the book have been supplied by Author and are the exclusive property of Author. Writer acknowledges access to certain of Author's trade secrets.

Writer shall be responsible only for writing a manuscript fit for submission to publishers. The work and expense of finding a market for it shall be undertaken by Author.

Writer shall submit a manuscript which is satisfactory to Author in form and content. Acceptability of the written works shall be at the sole discretion of Author. Work may be stopped at any time by Author.

Work timetable: (see example in Chapter Seven)

Fees. For completing the manuscript, in form fit for submission to publishers, Author will pay Writer the total sum of _____ dollars. The manner of payment shall be as follows:

1. On completion of this agreement, and before commencement of the work, an advance of _____ dollars.

2. On completion of the first draft, _____ dollars.

3. On completion of the second draft, _____ dollars.

4. On completion of the final draft, _____ dollars.

5. On completion of proofreading and indexing, _____ dollars.

6. And any previously approved, mutually agreed upon expenses.

These fees are full and complete and Writer fully understands there will be no further compensation or royalties.

This is a work for hire in which Author owns all copyright interests, and Writer assigns all of same to Author.

This contract shall run for the copyright life of the book and is binding on Author's and Writer's heirs, successors and assigns.

This contract is being entered into in good faith. It is the only agreement for this book between Author and Writer.

(signed)

Author: _____

Writer: _____

Date: _____

If your collaboration is between two more-or-less equal partners (e.g., co-authors), use the work agreement as an outline to make sure you have addressed all the important issues in your contract. Now let's discuss some of the items mentioned in the draft agreement.

CREDITS OR BILLING. How will the authorship of this book be listed on the cover and in all the book directories? Is your collaborator a true co-author or a ghost?

"The courts are full of people litigating verbal agreements. People have very selective memories when partnership trouble starts." - Jim Comiskey in *How to Start, Expand & Sell a Business.*

Allison Author

Allison Author with the assistance of Wendell Writer

Allison Author as told to Wendell Writer

Allison Author with Wendell Writer

Allison Author and Wendell Writer

Wendell Writer and Allison Author

There is no hard and fast rule on billing, but a lot depends on who is contributing what and how much to the product. Generally, your writer should get billing or money. Ghostwriters usually do not receive name credit as they are supposed to be invisible. If you are paying top dollar, you are buying the billing for yourself. If the writer wants his or her name on the cover, the paycheck should be lower.

If this is simply a marriage between an expert who can't write and a writer without a book idea, turn this apparent weakness into an asset by listing each's qualifications in the book credits and describe the union as the perfect marriage.

FLAT FEES OR ROYALTIES Should contributors get a percentage of the book or be paid a flat fee? Obviously flat fees are simpler and occasionally cheaper. Generally, a person creating a major portion of the book should get royalties while someone doing basic research, typing or contributing a drawing should be paid a set fee.

If you require a few drawings, go to a graphic artist and have them drawn to order. Then pay the bill and be done with it. The artist deserves a piece of the action no more than the person who painted your car before you sold it. Children's picture books require extensive illustrations so the artist usually splits the royalties with the author.

If you hire an artist to make a major contribution to your book, obtain a written release and assignment to any copyright he or she might have. Many authors negotiate a lower price for art by buying the right to use it in their book (present and future editions) only. The artist is free to peddle the illustrations elsewhere outside the book trade. The same is true for photographs.

DRAFT ARTIST RELEASE

    This is to confirm the understanding that I,_____, have   (taken photographs, provided artwork, etc.) for a book tentatively titled _____by: _____ (Author).

    All rights in and to the (photographs or artwork), including the copyright and renewal and extension of copyright on these (photographs or artwork) shall belong to Author, and I assign all said copyright interests to Author. My contributions are works for hire in which I retain no copyright interest.

    Author shall have the right to use my name in sales promotion or advertising of the work.

Name:_____

Witness:_____

Date: _____

    Co-authors usually split advances and royalties based on their predicted contributions to the manuscript. Expert/ writer teams either split royalties or the writer receives a flat fee. Ghosts will write a book for $2,000 to $6,000. But, if you are famous and the book is to be sold to a publisher, the ghost may perceive it to be in his or her interest to ask for up to 50 percent of what the book earns. If you plan to self-publish, or the sales are not projected to be too great, the ghost may want a flat fee. Royalty reports are a time-consuming chore which may be avoided if you pay a flat rate for material received.

AMOUNT OF COMPENSATION—Here are some hourly rates to guide you in hiring editorial and other services. Prices vary from region to region and are for 1985. These are commercial rates, fees charged by those who have overhead. Some moonlighters and freelancers may work for less. These figures are not firm and are presented here mainly for comparison.

SERVICE	HOURLY RATE
Research	$13.00
Discovering facts and material to be used by the author.	
Ghosting	$2-6,000/book
Contract writing. You may pay your writer on a per-book, per-page or per-hour basis. The per-page or per-book ("piecework") provides you with a better idea of total project cost. The writer should also be reimbursed for expenses.	
Manuscript typing	$1.25/page or $15.00/hour
Straight typing, double-spaced page.	
Copy editing	$10.00
Checking for grammar, punctuation and style.	
Peer review	$50-$150/book (honorarium)
Having another expert review the book for technical accuracy. Many will not charge to check over a chapter.	
Content editing	$12.00
Fact checking and material presentation.	
Rewriting	$15.00
Cleaning up the writing while retaining the author's material, approach and style.	
Fact checking	$15.00
Verifying statements, statistics and facts.	

Proofreading $8.00
    Reading galleys or bluelines against a man-
    uscript word for word to check for typos,
    word divisions and paste-up problems.

Editorial proofreading $8.00
    Proofing for continuity of style.

Indexing $1.00-$1.25/book page
    Preparing the book's index.

Project development $15.00
    Supervising the whole project from idea
    through production.

Paste-up $5.00-$20.00/page.
    Graphic arts work. Price varies with complexity.

Creative design $30.00
    Designing and specifying typefaces, paper,
    illustrations and layout.

Cover copywriting $95.00/cover, up
    Flat fee for front and back cover sales copy.

Photographs, existing $3-$20.00
    Black and white print, 5 x 7
    Agency fees are $125.00 for ½ page black
    and white.

Photographs, shot to order $50.00 and up,
    Black and white print, 5 x 7 depending on quantity.

Illustrations, each $200 for ¼ page b/w, $250 color.
    $500 for full page b/w, $750 color.

Line drawings for the interior of book. $15-$25, including type.
    Simple graphs and charts,The more crea-
    tive the art, the more it costs.

Cover art $900.00
    Four color including art, type and ready for
    color separations.

THE ADVANCE paid to your writer seals the deal, which is an important legal consideration. It also puts pressure on both of you to perform. The advance makes the writer feel accepted and has great psychological value; the advance does not have to be large to work as an incentive.

Advances generally range all the way from $100 to $5,000 and are usually in the area of 20 to 25 percent of the total. One way to create an incentive, or at least to make the writer feel continually obligated, is to make progress payments. One-fifth may be paid on signing the contract, one-fifth when the writer submits the first draft, one-fifth when he or she completes the second draft and so on.

THE ROYALTY FORMULA, traditionally, has been for the publisher to pay the author 10 percent of the list (cover) price for each hardcover book sold through regular channels such as book wholesalers, book stores and libraries. Or graduated royalties for the hardcover edition might be 10 percent of the list price on the first 5,000 books sold, 12½ percent on the next 5,000 and 15 percent on sales over 10,000. Often softcover authors command 7 percent for the first 12,000 sold and 9 percent above that number. The royalties on textbooks are generally 15 percent of net (the cover price, less 20 percent). It is common in college text publishing for royalties to jump to 18 percent of net over a certain number sold.

If two people write the book, they split the royalties. However, you could buy all rights from your collaborator and avoid paying the split.

SUBSIDIARY RIGHTS Most contracts call for the author and publisher to split the subsidiary rights (films, book clubs, etc.) 50-50. Many contracts give the author 50 percent for print-reproductions and 90 percent of the nonprint-adaptations. Many of the big publishers barely break even on the book itself and hope to make their money on the subsidiary rights.

Unless you have a narrow field of interest or the author has very strong feelings about a particular rights area, you will want a contract which includes all possible reprint rights. Once you have published the basic book, you will want to entertain the possibilities of translations to other languages or co-publishing in other English-speaking markets. Then there are book club adoptions, film rights, magazine excerpts, newspaper serializations and the mass market paperback rights. Your promotion will rub off on all areas, so make the most of your efforts by taking complete control of the manuscript.

COPYRIGHT CLEARANCES or permissions are the responsibility of the writer (unless you have supplied the material) and this should be spelled out in the contract. The writer knows his or her sources better than you and should be responsible for obtaining permission for extracted material, articles, photos or drawings. This includes the right to translate foreign material.

TERM AND CONTINUITY OF THE CONTRACT The agreement may be for a stated period, say the completion of the manuscript, or for the copyright life of the book. It should be made binding on those who succeed both sides: the heirs and so on.

SCHEDULE Include a work timetable and a clause allowing you to cancel the agreement if the writer fails to meet deadlines; always keep the pressure on writers to perform. Your writer must turn in work regularly while you must edit it promptly.

Use written memos to convey deadlines. A memo avoids misunderstandings and may be used as evidence should there be a dispute later.

KEEP FINAL SAY Whether you are dealing with an editor, co-author, researcher or ghostwriter, retain final approval as to acceptability of the product produced by your partner. Product acceptability may be worded "in form and content satisfactory to the author" (you). This may sound a bit harsh as it can be very subjective but someone has to steer the ship. It is your job to maintain control of all aspects of the project. Just because your partner in this work is an expert at writing does not mean he or she knows better than you what should be in your book. You are paying the bill and you must get what you want. You may not always be right but you are always the boss.

Publishers routinely contract for books and pay advances with the understanding that the author is obligated to turn in an "acceptable" manuscript. So do not feel uncomfortable about retaining final approval. To be fair to the writer and to your project, you will probably be better off giving progressive approval, chapter by chapter.

Final say as to acceptability must be made clear at the time of the contract negotiation because you are dealing with egos. If your partner understands you have final say, he or she is less likely to sulk when you cut or change the work. Final say must be discussed during negotiation and be part of the contract. Retaining final approval is usually less of a problem when dealing with a professional writer.

If you cannot agree on the work or changes, you have the right to remove the writer from the project while the writer has the right to keep all progress payments received.

FURTHER CLAUSES include arbitration agreements in case of dispute, a paragraph saying the contract is being entered into on the basis of "good faith" and a statement that this is the only agreement, that neither party is bound by any other discussion during the negotiations.

WORKS FOR HIRE So-called "works (done) for hire" under the Copyright Act belong to the employer. The hired writer has no copyright interest in the material. The writer, though, can retain the copyright or a share in it if it is so specified in the employment contract, or other written agreement.

The scope of the definition of "work for hire" is very complex. Under copyright law the question of who is considered an employee is not very clear. The courts' decisions on this subject have been contradictory. In every case an agreement should be signed between employer/employee that clearly delineates who owns what copyright interests. This exercise will avoid later complications.

Collaborators who normally do not have any copyright interest in the end-product include persons whose work is merely research, editing, proofing, pasting-up, or a contribution to a collection, a translation, a supplementary work, a compilation, or persons who prepare textbook material or tests, according to the Copyright Act. But, if the writer's contribution is important enough, he can bargain for a share of the copyright interest, and reduce that to a written agreement. That is an enforcable contract right.

Writers who are commissioned or hired as independent contractors to work on a book or other work, including ghostwriters, are not traditional employees or hired-hands. They are more creative forces who normally have copyright interests in what they produce. Again, this can be varied totally or in part by a written agreement.

In addition to the agreement, copyright interests may be established as follows: The copyright owner may sell, release, or transfer in writing all or part of his or her rights. Or, separate licensing agreements for limited use may be contracted, which should also be registered in the Copyright Office.

As the author of a book, you may want to buy outright, or in part, any copyright interest those persons working with you may have. Then, protect that purchase by registering yourself with the copyright office as the owner, explaining on the form how you acquired ownership of the copyright. Obtain the current form from the Copyright Office, Library of Congress, Washington, DC 20559.

4 SPACE 4: Claimant(s)

Name(s) and Address(es) of Copyright Claimant(s): Give the name(s) and address(es) of the copyright claimant(s) in this work even if the claimant is the same as the author. Copyright in a work belongs initially to the author of the work (including, in the case of a work made for hire, the employer or other person for whom the work was prepared). The copyright claimant is either the author of the work or a person or organization to whom the copyright initially belonging to the author has been transferred.

Transfer: The statute provides that, if the copyright claimant is not the author, the application for registration must contain "a brief statement of how the claimant obtained ownership of the copyright." If any copyright claimant named in space 4 is not an author named in space 2, give a brief, general statement summarizing the means by which that claimant obtained ownership of the copyright. Examples: "By written contract"; "Transfer of all rights by author"; "Assignment"; "By will." Do not attach transfer documents or other attachments or riders.

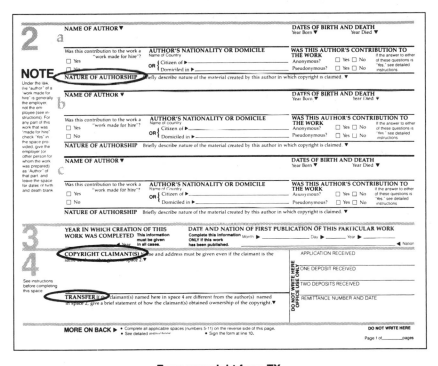

From copyright form TX

The above suggestions reflect current law, but are not intended as legal advice for your specific situation. You should consult a literary attorney to help with the written documents.

DRAFT ASSIGNMENT OF COPYRIGHT

This assignment of copyright is made between_____
(the Writer) and _____
_____(the Author).

Whereas, the Writer has created an original work titled
_____
and is the sole proprietor of the copyright in such work, and

Whereas, the Author wishes to acquire the entire interest of the
Writer in said work,

Now, therefore, in consideration of $_____,
the receipt of which is hereby acknowledged, the Writer hereby assigns
and transfers to Author, his heirs, executors, administrators, and assigns,
all of Writer's right, title, and interest in the said work and the copyright
thereof throughout the world, including any statutory copyright together
with the right to secure renewals and extension of such statutory copyright throughout the world, for the full term of said copyright or statutory
copyright and any renewal or extension thereof which is or may be
granted throughout the world.

In witness whereof, Writer has executed this instrument as of the
day and year set forth below.

Name:_____

Witness:_____

Date:_____

Example of Assignment of Copyright

(It would be advisable to sign this assignment before a Notary
Public or witness, though this is not strictly required by law.)

CONFLICT RESOLUTION Even with a tightly written contract, the way the project was conceptualized and the way the work proceeds may be very different. The two most common problems between collaborators involve who should be listed as the first author and how the income from the book should be split. As the project proceeds, one partner may feel that she or he is contributing more than a fair share, while the other partner is to receive top billing. When conflicts surface, decide first whether discussing them is worth unsettling the partnership and slowing progress on the manuscript. Conflict can kill initiative and creativity. If you decide to broach the subject, try to settle the problems by talking them through. Then if you change some of your original plans, make the needed alterations in your contract and responsibility chart.

If the problem is more serious, you might want to bring in an outside facilitator or arbitrator. Make sure this is someone neither of you know, but someone familiar with the publishing profession. You and your partner have come a long way together. It would be a shame to give up on your project now.

No matter how well you plan, conflict can arise during the writing process. It is important to settle conflicts immediately, so they do not get in the way of your mission. Talk to each other, don't just stew over the problem.

You and your partner must be fair to the project as well as to each other. You must agree not to raise partnership issues just prior to a deadline. This valuable time must be spent on the manuscript, not in arguing.

For more partnership information and a sample collaboration agreement, get a copy of the book *Author Law & Strategies* by Brad Bunnin and Peter Beren.

Now that you are committed to a writing partner, the next question is, can you accept the stresses of authoring?

"Discussion is an exchange of knowledge; argument an exchange of ignorance." - Robert Quillen

"In contracts, the big print giveth and the small print taketh away."

15

WRITING AND YOUR PERSONAL LIFE

For many people, writing a book is a stressful time. Tempers run short, relationships are strained and sleep is fitful. Some authors turn to pills or drink to help them cope with their situation. Some find their resistance to colds and other communicable diseases is lower during this time. What is so stressful about writing a book? Here are what some authors say:

> "Writing is a very solitary endeavor. It is a tedious effort that requires total concentration."

> "The permanence of the written word in a book makes you vulnerable. A bad review can not only ruin your sales but it can undermine your self-esteem."

> "You have to be able to take criticism for a creative work that you have spent months or even years completing. You know this while you are writing."

> "As you get closer to the completion of your work there is an inablility to think about anything else. You become addicted to getting it done. It puts a strain on your relationship and your health."

"I've given my memoirs far more thought than any of my marriages. You can't divorce a book." - Gloria Swanson

"I tend to punish myself mentally until I get it down on paper."

"Writing? Oh it's easy—just sit down at your keyboard and open up a vein."

Remember not all stress is negative. The adrenaline rush that stress creates also helps your mind and body operate at their peak. Stress may be affecting your writing adversely if:

- You make every excuse you can to keep from sitting down at your keyboard.
- Any small distraction breaks your train of thought and you give up for the day.
- You are tense and irritable with those around you... family, friends, and colleagues.
- You can't relax and you are not sleeping well.
- You are over-indulging in food, cigarettes, alcohol or drugs.
- You wish you had never started this project.

If you find these things happening to you, you know it is time to take a break from the project, from a few days to a few weeks. It is time for a fresh perspective.

Many first-time authors are also holding down a full-time job. They find there simply is not enough time to do everything they would like. Attention to personal needs is one of the first things to go in a busy life, and eliminating this time for reflection and relaxation is truly stress-inducing. Be sure to exercise regularly and give yourself some personal time.

WRITER'S BLOCK is a common problem for most writers. Usually the frustration comes when you cannot get what is in your mind down on paper.

When you get a bad case of writer's block and thinker's cramp, admit to yourself that you do not know what you want to say and remove yourself from the project to think. This might only require taking a shower or running around the block. Or it could mean taking a vacation. Another technique is to switch to an easier part of the book. Creativity cannot be forced.

> *Mindy Bingham's book* Choices *was nearly complete in August, 1982. The only chapter left was the last one and it needed to be very creative to bring together what had been said. Mindy was stumped because she knew what she wanted to accomplish but not how. She took off on a five week tour of Europe and left the manuscript at home. At times while driving through the countryside a thought or an idea would pop into her head. When she returned she developed the exercises and wrote the final chapter in less than two hours.*

The best solution for stress and writer's block is to follow the organization in the book. Keep your manuscript in a binder, use the "pilot system" and work on the smallest and easiest areas first.

NEGOTIATING WRITING TIME WITH FAMILY, FRIENDS, EMPLOYERS AND YOURSELF You must sit down with your family or others who are used to claiming a large percentage of your time and discuss your project and how it will affect your relationships.

Before you begin your book, negotiate writing time and writing space. Then go over your timetable so they understand just how long this project should take. An author needs all the support he or she can get. Rumpled feelings from those in the support system will only create an emotional burden which will be counterproductive. You will have to become sensitive to the feelings of isolation from your loved ones as they view with jealousy your new "love affair"—your manuscript.

> "I have a sign on the door that says: *DO NOT COME IN. DO NOT KNOCK. DO NOT SAY HELLO. DO NOT SAY I'M LEAVING. DO NOT SAY ANYTHING UNLESS THE HOUSE IS ON FIRE...also, telephone's off!"* - Judith Krantz.

It might be helpful to share the following message with those close to you before you begin:

MESSAGE TO THE LOVED ONES OF AN AUTHOR

This writing project will cost you the time and the attention of 'your author'. Writing a book takes a tremendous amount of concentration, dedication, and time. If there are times you seek attention but 'your author' seems somewhere else, he or she probably is. The creative spirit and energy required to finish a book-length manuscript are all-consuming.

But this will not last forever. The book will get done. And then you can bask and delight in the limelight along with 'your author' because everyone will realize that without your support, understanding, and encouragement the book could never have been completed.

Have you ever wondered why most authors dedicate their books to spouses and children? You will soon find out why!

Mindy and Dan

HUSBAND/WIFE TEAM Sometimes it makes sense to involve a spouse with the project. He or she may be an equal co-author or may serve a supporting role in editing, typing or research. Working together can be beneficial to a marriage. Rather than suffering the stress resulting from dividing time between spouse and project, the project becomes something to work on together.

Negotiate a contract with your spouse the same way you would with an outsider. Not only must your roles be clear, you must agree on the time and personal commitment the book writing will receive. At this point, the potential of your writing is unknown, but earnings could turn out to be substantial. A contract now could alleviate problems with heirs (paricularly in the case of second marriages) in the event of a divorce or death.

It is advisable to work through the responsiblity chart in Chapter Thirteen. Clearly separate your writing lives from your personal lives. Avoid allowing professional disagreements to spill over into your personal partnership. Just because you disagree on a word, phrase or explanation, it does not follow that you love each other less.

Dr. Heather Johnston Nicholson and Dr. Ralph L. Nicholson wrote Distant Hunger: Agriculture, Food and Human Values *in 1979. Both were interested in the subject but each had a different orientation. Heather was a humanist and taught administration of public policy and Ralph was a scientist with a background in biochemistry and botany.*

They decided to take one summer to work on the book. The Nicholsons set limitations on the project by defining the study as the only workplace. The rest of the house was off limits to their project-related discussions.

The Nicholsons complemented each other in this work. Because the book was to be addressed to the layperson, they had to find a common language that could be understood by all. It became clear when there was too much social science jargon because Ralph couldn't understand it. They knew when they were using too many biological terms because Heather couldn't understand.

During that summer they developed a deep appreciation for each other's minds and a determination to understand each other's work. Where before they had a "low contention marriage," they now gave themselves permission to disagree as professional colleagues who were seeking truth. This changed approach brought them closer together and strengthened their marriage.

TELLING FRIENDS   It is a good idea to tell your close friends what you are doing. Do not expect them to understand the incredible time and energy commitment a book-length manuscript requires. But they will begin to notice that you do not have as much time for them now. Let them know the condition is temporary.

Do not tell everyone about your project. The more people you tell about your book, the more pressure you put on yourself to produce. Pretty soon everyone who sees you will want to know how the book is coming. While talking about your topic may give you practice in presentation as well as help in formulating your thoughts, be careful not to overdue this. Save your creative energy—you don't want to talk your subject to death.

Always remember that writing books is a competitive field. Do not give your good ideas away. Do not discuss your project with other authors, especially if you are producing a pathfinding book. The cocktail party is a good place to gather information, not to reveal it.

WRITING AND YOUR EMPLOYMENT Most first-time authors are also employed full-time. If you have a nine to five job this means you will have to work your writing time around these hours. Even when you are writing on your own time, there are pluses and minuses in telling your employer what you are doing. Here are just a few:

The minuses:

1. Some employers may be threatened by your project because if your book is successful you will no longer need conventional work and may leave the company.

2. Many employers do not like their employees to moonlight. They want all your energies. Anytime you are not in top

> "I just think it's bad to talk about one's present work, for it spoils something at the foot of the creative act. It discharges the tension." - Norman Mailer

mental form they may imagine it is due to a late night of writing.

3. Your work may be threatening to colleagues. A successful book may increase your status in the company and fellow employees may be jealous.

4. If you are writing about things you have learned in your company, your employer may feel some ownership of the material. Or, your employer may be afraid you are giving away trade secrets.

The pluses:

1. An employer could feel that your efforts are teaching you new skills and information, making you a more valuable employee.

2. A book establishes you as an expert and brings prestige to your company.

3. Your book will allow you to fullfill a dream and therefore make you a more contented person.

Weigh the pluses and minuses along with the temperament and policies of your employer before you reveal your new project. You may want some understanding and support during the months ahead and you may wish to ask for a short leave when you get down to the final draft.

WRITING RETREATS As you get close to the final draft of your book you will probably be less tolerant of distractions. After all, you are trying to keep an entire manuscript in your mind. This is a good time to take a quiet vacation. Or, consider a sabbatical or a leave without pay to complete your work.

For many people getting away from all distraction is probably the most efficient thing to do at this stage of the

---

"If you have two jobs and you're rich you have diversified interests. If you have two jobs and you're poor, you're moonlighting."

project. There are writers' colonies and retreat houses. You can even check into a motel or resort to avoid distractions. Or just find a quiet room in your home, put up the 'do not disturb' sign, and take the phone off the hook. For the final phase, a retreat can make the difference between a good book and a great book.

AUTOGRAPHING BOOKS is something you will be asked to do both in person and by mail. It is surprising how many prolific authors have never given much thought to how they might autograph a book. Confronted with an admiring fan, they are suddenly at a loss for words. Most authors simply sign: "To Wendy with best wishes," add their signature and sometimes the date. Try to be more personal. If there is something special about the buyer, include it in your autograph. Sometimes time does not permit more than a quick signature. But, on a mail order book, you can dream up something special. And, by the way, especially when rushed, make sure you spell your fan's name correctly. In all the hustle, it is easy to draw a blank and misspell the simplest name or word, ruining a book.

YOUR NEW STATUS. Your status will change from that of a private person, the "writer", to a public person, the "expert." You will have opportunities you never thought available until now. Your friends will treat you differently. Some will be happy for you and some will be jealous—jealous because they did not write the book. People new in your field will treat you like a god while those who have been around for years may be rather unkind.

> *Gary Glenn is a fire investigator. With his wife Peggy, they wrote a fire safety guide entitled* Don't Get Burned. *The new fire fighters treated Gary very specially while some of the old-timers felt threatened or were jealous.*

"A writer's life should be a tranquil life. Read a lot and go to the movies." - Mario Puzo

Many new authors who do write a book that gets a great deal of national notice do not foresee their new popularity, their celebrity status.

Bob Johnson co-authored the first book on the triathlon and was instantly propelled to celebrity status. While training for the "Iron Man" competition in Hawaii, he was pursued by groupies wherever he went.

Once you become a published author, your life will change. While the whole process might be exciting and stimulating, being in the limelight may not be as much fun as you used to dream.

In the meantime, let this chart suggest some solutions to the most common hazards of being an author.

THE HAZARDS OF BEING A SUCCESSFUL AUTHOR

HAZARDS	SOLUTIONS
Too much recognition	Use a pseudonym
Too many contacts	Get an unlisted phone
Jealous friends	Meet new people
Lost personal time	Say 'no' Hire help Quit your other job
Your book becomes your identity	Write a new book
Post publishing blues	Take a vacation Write a new book
Addiction to writing	Don't worry about it Write a new book

"A celebrity is a person who works hard all his life to become known, then wears dark glasses to avoid being recognized." - Fred Allen

There will be other problems. But there are many other solutions. Most authors agree that the rewards of being published far outweigh the stress. And if you can think of a job that doesn't come equipped with its own kind of problems, let us know.

"Failure is very difficult for a writer to bear, but very few can manage the shock of early success." - Maurice Valency

16

YOUR PUBLISHING OPTIONS

Once your book is written, you have to decide how to get it into print. Fortunately, there are several choices. Read about your options and then see the evaluation at the end of the chapter.

You may approach a large New York general publisher or a smaller specialized publisher. You may work with an agent or deal with a "vanity" press. If you decide to self-publish, you may go to a book printer, a regular printer who can manufacture books or you might get your own printing press. If you choose to go your own route, you will become one of the many "small presses." As you expand your list of titles, you may find yourself with a thriving business. With drive and desire, you could, one day, even become a major conventional publisher. Now let's take a look at the choices by starting with some definitions.

"PUBLISH" means to prepare and issue material for public distribution or sale or "to place before the public." The book does not have to be beautiful, it does not even have to sell, it needs only to be issued. Saleability will depend upon the content and the packaging.

A "PUBLISHER" is the one who puts up the money, the one who takes the financial risk. He or she has the book printed and then distributes it hoping to make back more money than has been invested. The publisher may be a big New York firm or a first-time author but he or she is always the investor.

A "BOOK" by international standards is a publication with at least 49 pages not counting the covers. The U.S. Post Office will accept publications with eight or more printed pages for "book rate" postage. Books should not be confused with pamphlets which have less than 49 pages, or periodicals. Magazines and newspapers are examples of periodicals. They are published regularly and usually carry advertising.

THE BOOK PUBLISHING INDUSTRY in the U.S. consists of nearly 13,000 firms by R. R. Bowker's count, but there are many thousands more publishers who do not bother to apply for a listing. For example, over 130 book publishers are located in Santa Barbara, California, but Bowker lists just 10 percent of these one- and two-person firms. About 100 publishers are considered to be the major companies and most of them are located in New York City. Altogether, more than 60,000 people are employed in book publishing in the U.S. Sales amount to nearly $9-billion per year for the over 600,000 active titles listed in *Books in Print*. Even though most of the titles are reprints of older books, the volume of brand new titles still amounts to about 100 each day for every day the bookstores are open.

THE BIG PUBLISHING FIRMS concentrate on books which anticipate audiences in the tens of thousands. Many houses were absorbed by much larger soap and oil companies in the 1970s but were sold in the early 1980s when they found book publishing was not as predictably profitable as other media. A look at the economics of big publishing will help us to better understand their problems. It has been estimated that some 350,000 book length manuscripts are written each year but that only 32,000 go into print. Many of the larger publishers receive 15,000 to 20,000 unsolicited manuscripts each year. Reading manuscripts takes an enormous amount of editorial time and a very high percentage of the submissions are poorly written or do not fit the publisher's line; they are a waste of editorial time. Simon and Schuster says it has published less than one percent of all the unsolicited manuscripts it has received and then with modest success.

The 9,000 bookstores do not have the shelf space to display all of the 40,000 new (original and reprint) titles published each year so they concentrate on the books that move the best. Consequently, most publishers figure that even after selecting the best manuscripts and pouring in the promotion money, only three books of ten will sell well, four will break even and three will be losers.

Ever wonder why all the books in the store have very recent copyright dates? They are seldom more than a year old because the store turns them over so fast. Shelf space is expensive and in short supply. The books either sell or they go back to the publisher. If one title doesn't move, it is replaced by another.

Most initial print runs are for 5,000 books. Then the title remains "in print" (available for sale) for about a year. If the book sells out quickly, it is reprinted and the publisher dumps in more promotion money. If the book does not catch on, it is pulled off the market and "remaindered" (sold off very cheaply) to make room for new titles. The publisher has a business to run; there is overhead to consider and bills must be paid.

The financial demands cause him or her to be terribly objective about the line. To many publishers, in fact, a book is a book. If they already cover a subject, they won't be interested in a new manuscript on the same topic. They already serve that interest and do not care that yours might be better. Many big publishers are not interested in whether it is a good book; they are under financial pressure to publish only books

"All of us enjoy being the hot publisher of the moment—and in paperback that designation can change every three weeks." - Susan Petersen, President Ballantine Books.

that will sell. Therefore, they concentrate on authors with good track records or Hollywood and political personalities who can move a book with their name. Only occasionally will they accept a well-written manuscript by an unknown and then it must be on a topic with a ready and massive audience. A published writer has a much better chance of selling than an unpublished one, regardless of the quality of the work.

Large publishers usually must sell close to 10,000 copies in hardcover to break even. They hope to make their money on subsidiary rights for the paperback edition, book clubs, or movie rights. They spend several thousand dollars on promoting most titles and often more than $50,000 on a blockbuster. This makes it tough on the small publisher with less volume who must compete on the basis of sales and cannot afford large scale promotion.

Publishers, like most business people, seem to follow the "80-20" principle. That is, they spend 80 percent of their effort on the top 20 percent of their books. The remaining 20 percent of their time goes to the bottom 80 percent of their line. Most books have to sell themselves to induce the publisher to allocate more promotion money.

The author will get a royalty of 5 to 15 percent usually on a sliding scale and the economics here are not encouraging. For example, a print run of 5,000 copies of a book selling for $8 will earn $40,000 and a 10 percent royalty on this is $4,000. That probably is not enough money to pay for all the time spent at your keyboard. The chances of selling more than 5,000 copies are highly remote because after a year or two, the publisher takes the book out of print. In fact, the publisher will probably report fewer sales because some books will be returned by the bookstores unsold.

If your manuscript is a blockbuster novel with potential sales in the millions, you may need a big publisher and they certainly want you. They will take care of all the printing and distributing. But if you think you can have your royalty checks sent to you in Bimini, you may be disappointed. Once a book

> *"The best and most businesslike way to write for money—and consistent publication—is to find out what editors want and try to produce it."* - Kay Haugaard.

is produced by a publishing house, authors are often expected to take an exhausting role in promotion. Many publishing houses will not even consider a "nonpromotable" author anymore. They are looking for personalities as well as writing talent.

But if you have written a nonfiction book, you may be asked to furnish sales leads. Whatever your book, you may be expected to go on tour. You may wind up doing most of the promotion yourself while losing control over the program. When sales drop off, you might want to buy the book and the remaining stock back from the publisher so you can pursue the marketing yourself. At this time you may also discover to your dismay that your contract provides that you must submit your next two manuscripts to this same publisher.

The big publishing houses provide a needed service but for many first-time authors they are unapproachable. Once in, the author does not get the best deal and getting out may be very difficult. To begin with, the publisher may keep the manuscript for months, and then reject it. If your book is accepted, it may be heavily edited, or the title may be changed. Publishers say that they have invested lots of time and money to find out what will sell, but in return for their knowledge you lose some control of your project.

Some people say that the big publishers are schizophrenic in their approach—the editorial side goes after "prestige" manuscripts, while the marketing people push what they think they can sell.

In other words, the fact that your book will probably not be accepted by one of these top publishers should not be considered a major tragedy.

If you are still interested in pursuing established publishers, give yourself the best possible chance by going about the submission professionally. Do not just ship off your manuscript. Write a two or three page query letter to publishers of like books, outlining your book and its intended market. Ask if they would like to see your project. And don't hold your breath.

> *"Someday I hope to write a book where the royalties will pay for the copies I give away."* - Clarence Darrow

There is a brighter side: there are small publishers and self-publishers who are closer to their market. They understand what the public wants to read.

THE SMALL PRESSES usually specialize in certain areas such as technical books, regional books, poetry, and so on. They are often new at the trade and have yet to expand out of one or two lines of books. One definition of a small press is a publisher with no more than 12 full-time staff members, issuing fewer than 25 titles per year for receipts under $400,000. Most "small presses" are much smaller.

Para Publishing reluctantly added its second employee after sixteen years. Each year, it ships some 50,000 copies of twenty new and revised titles for a gross in the low six figures.

Many small presses emerged from the anti-establishment movement of the sixties, their existence made possible by the introduction of newer, simpler, cheaper (offset) printing methods. They may be small or fairly large, but nearly all are specialized. Many people in the industry are attracted by the flexibility these publishers offer. As the firms flourish, some of these talented employees break away and start new small presses of their own. There are thousands of small presses and because of their relatively low overhead, they can produce their books much cheaper than the big publishers.

However, while the smaller publishers may be closer to their market, their royalty rates are the same and many do not promote a title much harder than a big publisher. Most authors will agree that small publishers are usually nice to deal with and provide good personal attention but they are faced with many of the same economic problems as the rest of the industry and do not always have the resources to combat them. To find a small press, consult Dustbook's *International Directory of Little Magazines and Small Presses* and *Literary Market Place*. Look for a publisher who specializes in your type of book. Do not take a business book to a cookbook publisher. He will not take it and would not know where to sell it if he did. You want a publisher who knows the market, one who can plug your book into his promotion/distribution system.

CO-OP PUBLISHING HOUSES have been formed in many areas. Usually three to ten people join together to share the work of editing, design, layout, typesetting, compilation and financing. Often these people contribute more labor ("sweat equity") than money to the publishing venture. A good article on this subject appeared in the August, 1978 edition of *Writer's Digest* magazine.

VANITY PUBLISHERS publish over 1,000 titles each year; a half-dozen firms produce about 70 percent of all the subsidized books. Many of these businesses advertise in the Yellow Pages under "Publishers." Vanity publishers offer regular publishing services, but the author invests the money. Under this arrangement, the author pays the full publishing (more than just printing bill) costs, receives 40 percent of the retail price of the books sold and 80 percent of the subsidiary rights, if sold. According to *The Wall Street Journal*, the cost is between $2,000 and $15,000 to get into print. Others say you can figure roughly on $30 per printed page.

The vanity publisher claims he will furnish all the regular publishing services including promotion and distribution. But according to *Writer's Digest*, vanity publishers usually do not deliver the promotion they promise and the books rarely return one-quarter of the author's investment.

The ads reading "To the author. . ." or "Manuscripts wanted by. . ." easily catch the eye of the author with a book-length manuscript. Vanity presses almost always accept a manuscript for publication and usually with a glowing review letter. They don't make any promises regarding sales and usually the book sells fewer than 100 copies. The vanity publisher does not have to sell any books because the author has already paid for the work. Therefore, vanity publishers are interested in manufacturing the book, not in editing, promotion, sales or distribution.

Since binding is expensive, the vanity publisher often binds a few hundred copies; the rest of the sheets remain unbound unless needed. The "advertising" promised in the contract normally turns out to be only a "tombstone" ad listing your book with many other titles in the *New York Times*. Results from this feeble promotion are rare.

The review copies sent by vanity presses to book reviewers usually go straight into the "circular file." They do not like vanity presses because they know the book has not been "accepted" by any third party. Further, they know from experience there will be little promotional effort and that the book will not be available to readers in the stores.

Only a local bookstore might be persuaded to carry an author's vanity press book. The rest know there won't be any promotional effort expended to bring the public in.

The vanity publisher can get your book into print if this is all you want and will not cut the manuscript all to pieces but, this is not the least expensive way to go. It would make more sense to contract with a book packager to handle the whole job or a book printer or even a regular local printer who has the equipment to print books. Publishing yourself should save 25 to 35 percent over vanity publishing.

Before considering a vanity publisher, send for *Does it Pay to Pay to Have it Published*? (Writer's Digest, 9933 Alliance Road, Cincinnati, OH 45242). From everything you read, it appears that no one likes vanity publishers. Some have been in trouble with the Federal Trade Commission (FTC) and at least one has been sued by a client author.

BOOK PRODUCERS are packagers who take your idea and then handle the writing, editing, illustrating, design, layout and printing. They deliver the books to you and you handle the marketing, billing and collecting. Many packagers specialize in certain areas such as children's books, so shop around. A list of book producers can be found in *Literary Market Place*.

"What an agent is supposed to do is ensure there is a competitive spirit when a publisher buys a book." -Theron Raines, agent.

LITERARY AGENTS provide a valuable service to publishers by screening out the not-yet-ready manuscripts. Most new material comes to big publishers through them. Agents have to serve the publisher well for if they submit a poor manuscript, the publisher will never give them another appointment. Therefore, agents like sure bets too, and are reluctant to even consider an unpublished writer. When they do, their fee is often higher than their normal commission of 10 to 15 percent.

For the author, agents will make manuscript suggestions, negotiate the contract and try to sell the book to one of their many contacts; agents will exploit all possible avenues. If your manuscript is a winner, it is wise to have professional management.

According to *Literary Agents '83-'84 Marketplace* about 40 percent of the book agents will not read manuscripts by unpublished authors and a good 15 percent will not even answer query letters from them. Of those agents who will read the manuscript of an unpublished author, 80 percent will charge for the service. 80 percent of the agents will not represent professional books; 93 percent will not touch reference works; 99 percent will not handle technical books; 98 percent will not represent regional books, satire, musicals and other specialized manuscripts. While most agents will handle novel-length fiction, only 20 percent are willing to take on either novelettes or short stories, and only 2 percent have a special interest in literature or quality fiction.

On the fringe, there are a number of "agents" who charge a "reading fee" and then pay students to read and critique the manuscript. They make their money on these fees, not from placing the manuscripts.

You may contact agents by mail. Send a query letter and a two to three page synopsis. The letter should describe the book, its intended market, describe your background and request permission to send the entire manuscript. For a list of literary agents, see *Fiction Writer's Market* and *Literary Market Place*. Also write for a list to The Society of Authors' Representatives (P.O. Box 650, New York, NY 10113). Agents specialize, so look for one who handles your type of book.

Must reading for anyone approaching an agent or conventional publisher is *How To Get Happily Published* by Judith Appelbaum and Nancy Evans.

PUBLISHING OPTIONS

Consider the following statements to help decide which publishing option is best for you.

Conventional publisher If you feel:

1. It is important to me to be published by a major New York publisher because I value the type of recognition that would bring.

2. I have a personal connection with a publisher. I know an editor and can get my manuscript considered.

3. Publishers and their editors will change my manuscript for the better. I trust their judgment.

4. I will be happy to accept a 10 percent royalty.

5. Rejection does not bother me. I will keep sending out my manuscript until I find the right publisher.

Then start trying to find a conventional publisher.

Vanity press If you feel:

1. I want a few copies of my book for family and friends. It does not have to sell.

2. I am not concerned about price or about getting a return on my investment.

3. I do not want to produce my own book.

Then a vanity press might serve your purposes well.

Book producer or packager If you feel:

1. I want an attractive, professional-looking book.

2. I want someone else to handle the details; to take my manuscript and deliver the books to me to sell.

A book producer might be your answer.

Agent If you feel:

1. I do not have the time to find a publisher.

2. I would rather create than sell.

3. I am confident of my talent as a writer.

You should try to find an agent.

Self-publishing If you feel:

1. I am business-like as well as creative.

2. I can afford to invest in a business.

3. I want to maintain complete control over my book.

4. If I wait much longer, someone else will beat me to the market.

5. I want a business of my own and I am willing to put in the time and effort necessary.

6. I want to maximize the return on my efforts.

Self-publishing might be the route for you.

Which option matches your skills and meets your needs? If you select self-publishing, you will be especially interested in the next chapter.

> *"When one door closes, another opens, but we often look so long and regretfully upon the closed door, we do not see the ones which open for us."* - Alexander Graham Bell

17
SELF-PUBLISHING

IN SELF-PUBLISHING, the author bypasses all the middle-men, deals directly with the printer and then handles the marketing and distribution. He or she maintains complete control over the product. The self-publisher invests time as well as money, but the rewards are greater. The self-publisher gets it all.

Self-publishing is not new. It is almost a tradition. Many authors have elected to go their own way after being turned down by regular publishers. Others have decided to go their own way from the beginning. Well- known self-publishers include Mark Twain, Zane Grey, Upton Sinclair, Carl Sandburg, James Joyce, D.H. Lawrence, Ezra Pound, Edgar Rice Burroughs, Stephen Crane, Mary Baker Eddy, George Bernard Shaw, Edgar Allen Poe, Rudyard Kipling, Henry David Thoreau, Walt Whitman, Robert Ringer, Richard Nixon and many, many more.

IS YOUR BOOK A GOOD CANDIDATE FOR SELF-PUBLISHING? Some topics are especially likely to be successful in a self-published format. Your book might be if it is:

- Of interest to a specific group of people that you know how to reach.
- Likely to take a while to catch on with the public because it deals with a topic that is new or different.

- Of local or regional interest.
- Full of information needed by a certain group of people (cat owners, rose gardeners, do-it-yourselfers).
- Written specifically for your colleagues or your students.
- A philosophical or political treatise.

> *Since 1969, Dan Poynter has sold over a half-million copies of his books while Mindy Bingham's first book netted $112,000 in its first year. Naturally, they are strong advocates of self-publishing.*

There are thousands of small author/publisher firms, many of them in California. Small press publishing is not "poverty publishing." Some are growing and some are withering, but practically all are hanging on. They are proving that a self-published book is not inferior to one marketed by a big New York firm. Some self-publishers are very successful and some are making a lot of money.

Self-publishing is not difficult. In fact, it may even be easier than dealing with a publisher. The job of the publishing manager is not to perform every task, but to see that every task gets done. The self-publisher deals directly with the printer and handles as many of the editing, proofing, promotion, and distribution tasks as he or she can. What he can't do, he farms out. Therefore, self-publishing may take on many forms depending on the author's interests, assets and abilities. It allows you to concentrate on those creative and business areas you find most challenging.

Properly planned, there is little monetary risk in self-publishing. If you follow the plan, the only variable is the subject of the book. Poetry and fiction are difficult to sell but most nonfiction topics sell and can be profitable. In fact, many authors publish themselves because this method provides the best return on their labor. The big publisher only gives the

> "The cost of publishing a book is no more than the cost of a year in a good college and publishing a book _is_ a year in a good college."

book a short time to flourish or fail. The self-publisher, on the other hand, uses the first year to build a solid market for a future of sustained sales. While a big publisher may sell only 5,000 copies total, the self-publisher can often count on sales of 5,000 or more each year, year after year. Here are eight good reasons to self-publish:

1. **To make more money** Why accept six percent to ten percent in royalties when you can have as much as 40 percent? You know your subject and you know the people in the field. You may know better than some distant publisher where to find the buyers. While the trade publisher may have some good contacts, he may not know the market as well as you, and you are undoubtedly more committed to the book. Ask yourself this question: will the trade publisher be able to sell four times as many books as I can?

   The return for time invested becomes even more important when producing a highly technical work which has a small audience.

2. **Speed** Most publishers work on a one-and-a-half year production cycle. Can you wait that long to get into print? Will you miss your market? The 1½ years begins after the sale of the manuscript and all the contract negotiations. Publication could be three years away! Why waste valuable time shipping your manuscript around to see if there is a publisher out there who likes it? Richard Nixon self-published *Real Peace* in 1983 because he felt his message was urgent; he could not wait for a publisher's machinery to grind out the book.

   Typically, bookstores buy the first book to come out on a popular subject. Books published later may be better but the buyer might pass on them since the store already has the subject "covered." If your book is on a subject popular right now, you might want to self-publish.

> *"The oldest books are still only just out to those who have not read them."* - Samuel Butler

3. **To keep control of your book** According to *Writer's Digest*, sixty percent of the big publishers do not give the author final approval on copy editing. Twenty-three percent never give the author the right to select the title, twenty percent do not consult the author on the jacket design and thirty-six percent rarely involve the author in the book's promotion.

   The big New York trade publishers may have more promotional connections than you but with a whole stable of books to push, your book may get lost in the shuffle. At least, if you self-publish, you can be sure that your book is in the hands of someone who cares—you.

4. **Save your energy** Unless you are a movie star, noted politician or have a recognizable name, as a first time author it is nearly impossible to attract a big publisher.

5. **Self-publishing is good business.** There are far more tax advantages for an author/publisher than there are for authors.

6. **Self-publishing will teach you to think like a publisher.** You will learn the industry and will have a better understanding of the big picture. This can't help but make your manuscript stronger.

   A book is a product of one's self. An analogy may be drawn with giving birth. The author naturally feels that his book is terrific and that it would sell better if only his publisher would promote it more. He is very protective about his book (ever try to tell a mother her child is ugly?) The publisher answers that he is not anxious to dump more money into a book that is not selling. So, if the author self-publishes, he or she gains a better understanding for the arguments on both sides. It is his or her money and choice.

"Every imaginative production must contain some element of risk."
- Paul Horgan.

7. **You will gain self-confidence.** You will be proud to be the author of a printed book. Compare this feeling with pleading with people to read your manuscript.

8. **Finally, you may have no other choice.** There are more manuscripts than can be read. Most publishers will not even look at your manuscript. Just because your manuscript has not been read by a publisher does not mean it isn't worth publishing. Even a rejection slip after a reading is no sign of poor quality—your book may not fit their product line. If you know your field and are receiving positive feedback from your peers, you should go ahead and publish the book yourself.

SHOULD YOU SELF-PUBLISH? Would-be author/publishers should be cautioned that self-publishing is not for everyone. Writing is an art while publishing is a business and many people are unable to do both well.

In self-publishing, once the manuscript has been completed, the creative spirit must give way to the entrepreneur and the promoter. For some people, this is simply too schizophrenic. But for those who can make the transition, self-publishing is arguably the most satisfying and lucrative way to get into print.

Take the following quiz to help determine if you are a good candidate for self-publishing.

> *"An entreprenuer spends 16 hours a day to avoid having to work for someone else for eight hours."* - James Healey

SELF-PUBLISHING EVALUATION

Check the box that best describes you or your feelings.

Entrepreneurial spirit

☒ **1.** I like being in control. I like to have the final say on the direction of my projects.

☐ **2.** I like to have someone else make the final decisions after I give my input.

☐ **3.** I would rather be given direction and do not want too much responsibility.

Ability to risk capital

☐ **1.** I have money I can afford to risk in my business ventures.

☐ **2.** I'm willing to invest my time but not my money in my writing projects.

☒ **3.** I want assured compensation for my writing.

Ability to 'toot your own horn'

☒ **1.** I have something to share with others and I need to make sure they know about it.

☐ **2.** While I am a modest person, I know that books need promotion to sell so I will do it.

☐ **3.** I would have a hard time promoting my own work. It would seem like boasting.

Independence

☒ **1.** Most of all I want to be my own boss.

☐ **2.** While I consider myself independent I don't want to make all the decisions about the book by myself.

☐ **3.** Being on my own really scares me. I would rather have the security of being an employee and let someone else worry about the problems.

Time to promote your book

☒ **1.** I realize that writing a book is only the tip of the iceberg. I am ready for the time demands of promotion.

☐ **2.** I'll spend time on promotion but I don't want the major responsibility or time demands.

☐ **3.** All I want to do is finish the manuscript. I do not want to spend any more time on this project. I want to go on to something else.

Business acumen

☒ **1.** I consider myself realistic and "street wise" when it comes to business.

☐ **2.** Most business situations make sense, but there are areas where I need experience.

☐ **3.** I am inexperienced or impractical in business matters.

Public image

☒ **1.** I love to speak in front of audiences and feel I have something important to say.

☐ **2.** I need some confidence in public speaking and presence but I am willing to learn.

☐ **3.** I'm a private person. I do not want to make public presentations or be recognized in a crowd.

Goal oriented

☒ **1.** Once I know what I want, I cannot be distracted from my goal.

☐ **2.** I need someone to help me stay on track. Otherwise I take more detours than I should.

☐ **3.** I have a hard time deciding what it is I really want.

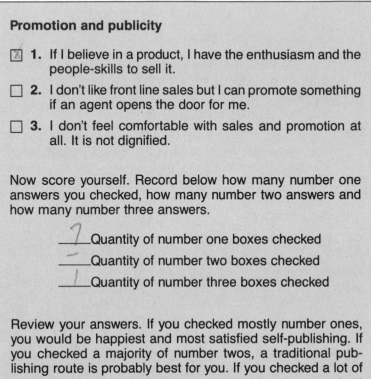

Promotion and publicity

☒ **1.** If I believe in a product, I have the enthusiasm and the people-skills to sell it.

☐ **2.** I don't like front line sales but I can promote something if an agent opens the door for me.

☐ **3.** I don't feel comfortable with sales and promotion at all. It is not dignified.

Now score yourself. Record below how many number one answers you checked, how many number two answers and how many number three answers.

_____1_____ Quantity of number one boxes checked

_____−_____ Quantity of number two boxes checked

_____1_____ Quantity of number three boxes checked

Review your answers. If you checked mostly number ones, you would be happiest and most satisfied self-publishing. If you checked a majority of number twos, a traditional publishing route is probably best for you. If you checked a lot of number threes you should reconsider authoring a book. If you want your book accepted beyond your immediate circle of family and acquaintances, it may be a very frustrating or negative experience for you.

This evaluation was written to identify your potential in producing a financially successful book. If your book is meant to be a family heirloom, just something you want to do for yourself, or a monument to your area of life study, you probably have no alternative to self-publishing.

Generally speaking, a large New York publisher may be more successful selling fiction while you may make more money publishing your own nonfiction. You must decide whether you wish to write, publish and/or make money.

It is possible to self-publish fiction or, at least, some people are doing it, but it isn't easy. Dorothy Bryant, a novelist in Berkeley, California, successfully publishes and promotes what she writes. She calls her publishing company Ata Books.

Fiction can also make money when published on a smaller scale according to a proven formula.

John Martin at Black Sparrow Press in Santa Barbara publishes only good fiction and poetry—defined as that fiction and poetry he likes. He has published many well-known authors and knows what he is doing, blending creative work with business. With years of experience, he can predict how his books will sell and has many standing orders. Each book is produced in a precise number of softcover, hardcover, deluxe, and signed editions. His success in selling fiction is so well-known, he maintains a post office box and an unlisted telephone number so authors cannot drop by or even call him.

You can take the author's royalty and the publisher's profit, all of the reward, by being both of them. Now, in addition to achieving the wealth and prestige of a published author, you can propel yourself into your own lucrative business: a publishing house. This shortcut not only makes more money (why share it?) but also saves you the time and trouble required to sell your manuscript to a publisher.

MAIL ORDER Today, more books are sold through the mail than through book stores. In fact, books are the leading mail order product. One-third of all these books are in the "how-to" category. Mail order is considered one of the best ways for the beginner to start a venture of his or her own. Selling books by mail is a good, solid day-to-day business opportunity.

Mail order is not only the simplest way to distribute books, it is an ideal way to build a second income or a new life. You do not have to give up your job, there is little overhead, there are tax breaks, you work for yourself and the business can be operated anywhere: you need only be near a post office. No one knows about your age, education, race or sex; your opportunities are indeed equal.

Mail order marketing is like fishing. You throw out a line by promoting your products and you find out almost immediately if you have made a sale. Everyday is like Christmas; opening envelopes and finding checks is great fun.

Initially, you will store your books in a closet and will slip them into padded bags for mailing. It is really quite easy and starting out is not expensive or time consuming.

Your writing/publishing/mail order company is actually combining three profitable fields and concentrating on only the best parts of each. A business of your own is the great American dream and it is still attainable. In your own business, you make the decisions to meet only those challenges you find interesting. This is not "goofing off," it is making more effective use of your time; "working smarter, not harder." You only have so much time, so make the most of it.

Running your own enterprise will provide you with many satisfying advantages. You should earn more money because you are working for yourself rather than sharing your efforts with someone else. You have job security and never have to worry about a surprise pink slip. If your writing is something you do in your spare time, you always have your regular job to fall back on. You start at the top, not the bottom, in your own company, and you work at your own pace and schedule. You will meet interesting people because as an author and publishing executive, they will seek you out.

In your own small business, if you decide to make it a fulltime job, you may work when and where you wish; you do not have to go where the job is. You can work 'til dawn, sleep 'til noon, rush off to Hawaii without asking permission: this is flexibility not available to the clock punchers.

A NOTE TO ACADEMICS "Publish or perish" is a phrase familiar to all academics who wish to be promoted within the university system. At many schools, whether or not you have

---

"Whenever you see a successful business, someone once made a courageous decision." - Peter Drucker.

published articles or, better yet, books, is an important consideration in determining tenure.

When queried about self-publishing, an eminent professor in a highly technical field who sat on the peer review committee for a major university responded quickly that self-published works are given little credence at review time. This is probably true in most schools. In further discussion with this professor about what a self-published work 'really is' and the advantages it has for the dissemination of important information, he began to look at the option in a different light. The discussion ended with him considering self-publishing the book he really wanted to write which had a much narrower audience than his publisher wanted to pursue.

Academic review committees must learn to judge books strictly on the written *review* the work receives by peers and in appropriate journals. Commerical publishers are in the business of making money. They make decisions on what is 'worthy' of publishing based on the size of the audience or, in other words, how many books they are going to sell.

If you are an academician who must 'publish or perish,' if you have a book inside you that will add to world knowledge and if you feel that your book will not be what you envisioned if you are forced to work with a commerical publisher, you should seriously consider self-publishing. But **first** be sure to educate your academic review committee about the advantages and credibility of self-publishing.

SELF-PUBLISHING AND CHARITABLE ORGANIZA-TIONS As funding for many charitable organizations is cut back, agencies are faced with a greater need to become self-sufficient. And publishing a book can be a terrific fund raiser. Every organization has staff members or volunteers with expertise or information the public is willing to pay for. Junior League cookbooks have supported many programs around the country. If your favorite charity is having financial prob-

---

"It is impossible for ideas to compete in the marketplace if no forum for their presentation is provided or available." - Thomas Mann

lems, you might consider helping it out by organizing, writing and publishing a book for it to sell. It beats having a bake sale!

> *Self-published,* Choices *netted $250,000 for the Girls Club of Santa Barbara in its first two years. The added income meant that the Girls Club could continue offering low cost childcare to needy families.*

SELLING OUT Many self-publishers find that once their books become proven money makers, the big publishers come to them with offers to print a new edition. Some authors use self-publishing to break into the big time. Others keep on self-publishing, keeping the work and the money to themselves.

Being an author/publisher sounds like a good life and it does make good business sense. Working for yourself requires organization and discipline but work doesn't seem so hard when you are counting your own money. To find out more about do-it-yourself book publishing, see *The Self-Publishing Manual* by Dan Poynter.

Well, what is the verdict? Are you ready to take the plunge? Is it time to get that "book inside you" out? All you have to do to start the process is make the decision and develop your plan.

If you decide to begin, we hope the "book inside you" will emerge like a butterfly from a cocoon—luminous, vibrant and ready to fly.

"A journey of a thousand leagues begins with a single step."
- Lao-tzu

PERSONAL DECLARATION

On this date, _____19 _____, I _____am
beginning my book with the working title of

_____.

My primary motive(s) for authoring this book is/are

_____

The audience for this book is _____
_____My projected timetable is:
      To complete the initial research by _____
      To complete the first draft by _____
      To complete the second draft(s) by _____
      To complete the third draft by _____
      To complete the final draft by _____

I have shared and discussed these plans with my family and/or loved ones and they sign below to acknowledge their support of this project:

signature: _____

signature: _____

signature: _____

signature: _____

I will/will not need to collaborate with partners.
      If I will, I need to locate : (circle the appropriate)
            Co-author(s)   Content editor
            Writing partner   Copy editor
            Ghostwriter   Typist/wordprocessor
            Contract writer   Other:

I am going to pursue the following publishing option(s): (circle appropriate)

> *Conventional publisher*
> *Small publisher*
> *Vanity press*
> *Book producer (packager)*
> *Agent*
> *Self-publishing*

I have to get the following resource books for further study:

> *Title*   *Author(s)*

_____

_____

_____

_____

_____

_____

_____

_____

I am fully aware that the authoring of a book takes a tremendous amount of time and hard work. I have the desire and the perseverence to complete this project. I am ready to accept the challenge.

> *signature*_____

"Always bear in mind that your own resolution to succeed is more important than any other one thing." - Abraham Lincoln

AFTERWORD

"We learn by doing" and your first book will be your hardest. "We learn by our mistakes" and, hopefully, through the use of this book your mistakes will be small ones. We hope it introduces and guides you to a richer, more rewarding life.

There are four books every author should read and keep in his or her library. They are *How to Get Happily Published* by Judith Appelbaum and Nancy Evans, *Author Law* by Brad Bunnin and Peter Beren, *The Self Publishing Manual* By Dan Poynter and *Write Right!* by Jan Venolia. These books may be found at your public library, at better bookstores or by ordering from Para Publishing on the order form in the back of this book. Then review the other resources we have listed in the Appendix and get those relating to your subject.

The first step, the next one, is up to you. We hope you take it. As you write, refer to this manual. As you learn the business, make notes in it. Let us know where this book may be improved. Tell us your experiences (you may find your story in future editions). When you do get that first book into print, please send us a copy—autographed, of course.

Mindy Bingham
Dan Poynter

"No horse has ever won a race it didn't enter."

APPENDIX

RESOURCES

To write, you must read. To read you must have the best books. Here is a list of books which cover various aspects of writing and publishing. You will want to have some books on your shelf as references.

We have grouped specialized writing and publishing books. The explanations are brief. It is assumed that if you plan to write a cookbook, for example, you will want to purchase all of the cookbook how-to's. Most books have resource sections and ideas that will lead you to more information. Do not be overly concerned with page counts. Some "shorter" books measure 8½ x 11 and some are hard cover.

The least expensive place to find dictionaries, style manuals, and other reference books is at used book stores.

HOW TO ORDER BOOKS Prices include shipping charges when known and are marked "ppd." Add applicable sales tax when ordering from publishers within your state. Ordering addresses of most publishers are given. Books from larger publishers will arrive much sooner if ordered through your local bookstore. Some books are available from Para Publishing. See the order blank. If you cannot find any book mentioned in the text, send a self-addressed, stamped envelope to Para Publishing, P.O. Box 4232-P, Santa Barbara, CA 93140-4232 for ordering information.

RESEARCHING

Finding Facts Fast: *How to Find Out What You Want and Need to Know,* by Alden Todd. Reading, interviewing, observing and reasoning. 123 pp. $3.95 Ten Speed Press, P.O. Box 7123, Berkeley, CA 94707.

Knowing Where to Look, *The Ultimate Guide to Research* by Lois Horowitz. How and where to find the information you want. 436 pp. $18.45 ppd. Writer's Digest Books, 9933 Alliance Road, Bldg. P, Cincinnati, OH 45242.

The Independent Scholar's Handbook, How to Turn Your Interest in any Subject into Expertise by Ronald Gross. Selecting a topic, researching, writing and publishing for those outside of the university. 261 pp. $9.30 Addison-Wesley Publishing Co.

WRITING

The Writer's Handbook by Sylvia K. Burack. Magazine article reprints on every type of writing with a market section of wants from magazine and book publishers. 788 pp. $22.95 The Writer, Inc. 120 Boylston Street, Boston, MA 02116.

Writer's Market. How and where to sell to book publishers. Lists. 900pp. $21.45 Writer's Digest Books, 9933 Alliance Road, Bldg. P, Cincinnati, OH 45242.

The Writing Business by CODA. A collection of articles with numerous illustrative stories. Very basic. 345 pp. $11.50 ppd. Poets & Writers, 201 West 54th Street, New York NY 10019

Writing Part-time for Fun and Money by Jack Clinton McLarn. Writing for magazines with sections on writing confessions, business, children's articles and script writing. 232 pp. $3.95 ppd. Enterprise Publishing Co., Two West 8th Street, Wilmington, DE 19801.

If I Can Write, You Can Write, by Charlie Shedd. Rules, tools, steps and tips. 152 pp. $13.45 ppd. Writer's Digest Books, 9933 Alliance Road, Bldg. P, Cincinnati, OH 45242.

Writing With Precision by Jefferson D. Bates. Step-by-step lessons with rules on how to write. Sections on writing reports and regulations. 226 pp. $7.95. Acropolis Books.

Overcoming Writing Blocks by Karin Mack and Eric Skjei. How to get organized with sections on business, student, technical and personal writing. 240 pp. $5.95. J.P. Tarcher/Houghton Mifflin.

Making Money with Words by Clement David Hellyer. Writing for various different markets. 262 pp. $5.95. Prentice Hall.

How to Write How-to Books and Articles by Raymond Hull. Researching, writing and collaborating. 204 pp. $10.45. Writer's Digest Books, 9933 Alliance Road, Bldg. P, Cincinnati, OH 45242.

Getting Published, A Guide for Businesspeople and Other Professionals by Gary S. Belkin. Turning ideas into saleable articles. 210 pp. $8.95. Wiley.

Silicon English, Business Writing Tools for the Computer Age by Darlene Frank. How to write better with a word processor. 213 pp. $12.95. Royall Press, P.O. Box 9022, San Rafael, CA 94912.

EDITING

Write Right! *A Desk Drawer Digest of Punctuation, Grammar and Style* by Jan Venolia. Essential writing reference. 127 pp. $4.45 ppd. Periwinkle Press, P. O. Box 694-P, Gualala, CA 95445.

The Chicago Manual of Style. Standard reference for authors, editors, and proofreaders. Preparing and editing copy. 738 pp. $30. University of Chicago Press.

FICTION

Guide to Fiction Writing by Phyliss A. Whitney. Planning and techniques. 133 pp. $12.95. The Writer, Inc. 120 Boylston Street, Boston, MA 02116.

The Creative Writer's Phrase Finder by Edward Prestwood.   Phrases describing just about everything the fiction writer can imagine. 364 pp. $17.95 ppd. ETC Publicatiions, P.O. Dwr. 1627-A, Palm Springs, CA 92263.

How to Enter and Win Fiction Writing Contests by Alan Gadney. Stories, books, scripts, with tips and a list of contests, grants & scholarships. 224 pp. $8.95 ppd. Festival Publications, P.O. Box 10180-P, Glendale, CA 91209.

POETRY

A Poets Guide to Freelance Selling by Kathleen Gilbert. A business approach to getting poems into print via freelance magazine sales. 28 pp. $3. ppd. Violetta Books, P.O. Box 15151, Springfield, MA 01115.

Poet's Guide to Getting Published. Free. American Poetry Association, P.O. Box 2279-P, Santa Cruz, CA 95063.

How to Enter Poetry Contests to WIN by Leiper. $4.60. The Inkling, P.O. Box 128-P, Alexandria, MN 56308.

Periodicals

Small Press Review. P.O. Box 100-P, Paradise, CA 95969.

CODA: Poets & Writers Newsletter 201 West 54th Street, New York, NY 10019.

NONFICTION

Tools of Nonfiction by Barbara J. Borders, et, al. A 38 lesson course in nonfiction writing. 338 pp. (8½ x 11, spiral bound) $29.95 ppd. Wm. C. Brown, Publishers, P.O. Box 539, Dubuque, IA 52001.

How to Enter and Win Nonfiction & Journalism Contests by Alan Gadney. Articles and books, tips and contests-grants lists. 224 pp. $8.95 ppd. Festival Publications, P.O. Box 10180-P, Glendale, CA 91209.

CHILDREN'S BOOKS

Writing Books for Children by Jane Yolen. How to write juvenile fiction and nonfiction with suggestions on how and where to send manuscripts. The afterword contains a list of further reading on children's books. 152 pp. $9.95 The Writer, Inc. 120 Boylston Street, Boston, MA 02116.

How to Write for Children and Young Adults by Jane Fitz-Randolph. Formula writing for articles, books and scripts in a textbook layout. $4.95. Harper & Row, M.O. Dept., 2350 Virginia Avenue, Hagerstown, MD 21740.

How to Write a Children's Book and Get it Published by Barbara Seuling. Writing and selling various types of children's books with resources. 191 pp. $13.95 The Scribner Book Companies, Inc. 115 Fifth Avenue, New York, NY 10003.

Writing Juvenile Stories and Novels by Phyllis A. Whitney. How to write by a prolific writer. 188 pp. $7.95 The Writer, Inc. 120 Boylston Street, Boston, MA 02116.

Writing for Children & Teenagers by Lee Wyndham. Writing formula for fiction and nonfiction. Marketing. Resources. A revised classic. 268 pp. $11.45 ppd. Writer's Digest Books, 9933 Alliance Road, Bldg P, Cincinnati, OH 45242.

MYSTERIES

Mystery Writer's Handbook by Lawrence Treat. Anthology of writing and selling chapters. 284 pp. $10.45 ppd. Writer's Digest Books, 9933 Alliance Road, Bldg P, Cincinnati, OH 45242.

SCIENCE FICTION

Notes to a Science Fiction Writer by Ben Bova. How to write science fiction. 178 pp. $6.95 Charles Scribner's Sons, New York.

Writing and Selling Science Fiction by The Science Fiction Writers of America. Anthology of helpful writing and selling information. 195 pp. $9.45 ppd. Writer's Digest Books, 9933 Alliance Road, Bldg P, Cincinnati, OH 45242.

ROMANCES

Writing and Selling the Romance Novel by Sylvia K. Burack. Fifteen romance writers address various aspects of writing and selling romances. The Market section lists publisher's guidelines for submissions. 149 pp. $9.95 The Writer, Inc. 120 Boylston Street, Boston, MA 02116.

How to Write Romance Novels That Sell by Marilyn M. Lowery. A step-by-step how-to with the formula for writing different types of romances. Promotion tips. The appendix lists romance publishers, recommended reading and writers' organizations. 236 pp. $12.95 Rawson Associates. 115 Fifth Avenue, New York, NY 10003.

Writing Romance Fiction by Helene Schellenberg Barnhart. How to write various types of romances. Selling, advice, success stories, resources. 272 pp. $16.45 ppd. Writer's Digest Books, 9933 Alliance Road, Bldg P, Cincinnati, OH 45242.

Periodicals

Romance Writers' Report. P.O. Box 1726, Fargo, ND 58107.

CONFESSIONS

How to Write and Sell Confessions by Susan C. Feldhake. Fiction and nonfiction confessions from wholesome to racy to pornographic. Describes types and outlines formulas. 105 pp. $10.95 The Writer, Inc. 120 Boylston Street, Boston, MA 02116.

Confession Writer's Handbook by Florence K. Palmer. Formula writing, tips and marketing for magazines, books and scripts. 173 pp. $11.45 ppd. Writer's Digest Books, 9933 Alliance Road, Bldg P, Cincinnati, OH 45242.

GREETING CARDS

A Guide to Greeting Card Writing by Larry Sandman. Anthology on all types of card writing. 242 pp. $9.45 ppd. Writer's Digest Books, 9933 Alliance Road, Bldg P, Cincinnati, OH 45242.

LIFE STORY

How to Write Your Own Life Story, A Step by Step Guide for the Non-Professional Writer by Lois Daniel. A guide with personal experiences told in the first-person. First taught as a college course. 172 pp. $7.95 Chicago Review Press, 820 North Franklin, Chicago, IL 60610.

How to Write Your Life Story and Sell it for Profit by James William Anna. Writing from experience and keeping records. 63 pp. $3.95 Anna Publishing, Inc. 500 St. Andrews Blvd., Winter Park, FL 32792.

How to Write Your Autobiography, Preserving Your Family Heritage by Patricia Ann Case. Unique autobiographical outline. An interview; just answer the questions. 112 pp. $4.95 Woodbridge Press, P.O. Box 6189, Santa Barbara, CA 93111.

Your Life Story, How to Write, Print, Publish and Sell it Yourself by Earlynne Webber. Self-discovery through writing of autobiography. How to write, print and sell your experiences. 154 pp. $9.95 ppd. Echo Publishing Co., 8865 Laura Lane, Beaumont, TX 77707.

How You Can Trace Your Family Roots by Ron Playle. Practical research how-to by someone who has done it. 32 pp (8½ x 11). $6.00 ppd. R & D Services, P.O. Box 644, Des Moines, IA 50303.

How to Tape Instant Oral Biographies by William Zimmerman. Interviewing tips and questions for capturing life stories on tape or film. 102 pp. $5.95 ppd. Guarionex Press, Ltd., 201 West 77th Street, New York, NY 10024.

How to Write the History of a Family, a *Guide for the Genealogist* by W.P.W. Phillimore. Research sources and techniques. Reprint of an 1887 book. 206 pp. $13.00 Gale Research, Book Tower, Detroit, MI 48226.

How to Write the Story of Your Life by Frank P. Thomas. Unique approach to memoir writing. Resources. 230 pp. $14.45 ppd. Writer's Digest Books, 9933 Alliance Road, Bldg P, Cincinnati, OH 45242.

How to Write and Sell Your Personal Experiences by Lois Duncan. How to write personal experiences and selling to various markets. 226 pp. $12.45 ppd. Writer's Digest Books, 9933 Alliance Road, Bldg P, Cincinnati, OH 45242.

Hilborn's Family Newsletter Directory. A list of 1,509 families publishing newsletters in their own name. Tips on starting a family newsletter and other fascinating genealogical information. 30 pp. $5 ppd. Hilborn Family Journal, 42 Sources Blvd, #52, Pointe Claire, PQ, H9S 2H9, Canada.

COOKBOOKS

So, You Want to Write a Cookbook! by Judy Rehmel. How to collect recipes, get organized, write, print, self-publish, and sell a cookbook. 99 pp. $6.95 Marathon International Publishing, P.O. Box 33008, Louisville, KY 40232.

How to Write a Cookbook and Sell it by Frances Sheridan Goulart. Writing a cookbook for sale to a publisher. 117 pp. $14.95 Ashley Books, Inc. 30 Main Street, Port Washington, NY 11050.

How to Publish and Sell Your Cookbook, a *Guide for Fundraisers* by George Beahm. The business side of cookbook publishing. 80 pp. $9.45 ppd. GB Publishing, P.O. Box 7359, Hampton, VA 23666.

How to Write a Cookbook and Get it Published by Sara Pitzer. Gathering recipes, writing, illustrating; publishing choices. Nicely illustrated. 253 pp. $17.45 ppd. Writer's Digest Books, 9933 Alliance Road, Bldg P, Cincinnati, OH 45242.

SCIENTIFIC/TECHNICAL

How to Write and Publish a Scientific Paper by Robert A. Day. How to organize, write, submit, print, etc. 160 pp. $17.95 ISI Press, 325 Chestnut Street, Philadelphia, PA 19106.

Essentials for the Scientific and Technical Writer by Hardy Hoover. Organization, tips and reference for technical writers with exercises. 216 pp. $4.00 Dover Publications, 180 Varick Street, New York, NY 10014.

The Technical, Scientific and Medical Publishing Market by Judith S. Duke. A market study detailing size, composition and trends. 218 pp. $34.95 Knowledge Industry Publications, 701 Westchester Avenue, White Plains, NY 10604.

COMPUTER

The Complete Guide to Writing Software User Manuals by Brad M. McGehee. Production mechanics. 165 pp. $16.45 ppd. Writer's Digest Books, 9933 Alliance Road, Bldg P, Cincinnati, OH 45242.

How to Write Computer Manuals for Users by Susan J. Grimm. A system to help the computer professional write a good manual the first time. 211 pp. $21.00 Lifetime Learning Publications, Ten Davis Drive, Belmont, CA 94002.

TRAVEL

Travel Writer's Markets by Elaine O'Gara. Tips, references and lists of book and magazine publishers who print travel material. Updated twice a year. 95 pp. $16.45 ppd. Winterbourne Press, P.O. Box 7548-C, Berkeley, CA 94707.

Periodicals

Travelwriter Marketletter by Robert Scott Milne. Sample $4. The Plaza Hotel #1745-P, Fifth & 59th Street, New York, NY 10019.

OUTDOOR BOOKS

Successful Outdoor Writing by Jack Samson. Writing for magazines, books and scripts. Fishing, shooting, camping, boating, etc. Examples. 244 pp. $13.95 ppd. Writer's Digest Books, 9933 Alliance Road, Bldg P, Cincinnati, OH 45242.

Part-Time Cash for the Sportsman by Jim Capossela. Writing books and other pursuits. 72 pp. $4.70 ppd. Northeast Sportsman's Press, P.O. Box 188, Tarrytown, NY 10591.

How to Write for the Outdoors Magazines by Jim Capossela. Directed toward magazine articles but useful in book writing. 72 pp. $4.70 ppd. Northeast Sportsman's Press, P.O. Box 188, Tarrytown, NY 10591.

REGIONAL BOOKS

Writing for Regional Publications by Brian Vachon. Writing for newspapers, magazines and books. Writing, photography and art. 203 pp. $13.45 ppd. Writer's Digest Books, 9933 Alliance Road, Bldg P, Cincinnati, OH 45242.

PHOTO BOOKS

Publish Your Photo Book by Bill Owens. Self-publishing for photographers. 143 pp. $8.95 Owens Publishing. Out of print. Check your library or try to find a used copy.

Sell & Re-sell Your Photos by Rohn Engh. What sells, where to sell and pricing. Resources. 323 pp. $16.45 ppd. Writer's Digest Books, 9933 Alliance Road, Bldg P, Cincinnati, OH 45242.

Starting and Succeeding in Your Own Photography Business by Jeanne C. Thwaites. Setting up and running a photo studio. 343 pp. $20.45 ppd. Writer's Digest Books, 9933 Alliance Road, Bldg P, Cincinnati, OH 45242.

FILM/TV/VIDEO/STAGE

Writing Television & Motion Picture Scripts That Sell by Evelyn Goodman. Formula for writing with an interesting inside look; historical Hollywood examples. 219 pp. $8.95 Contemporary Books, 180 North Michigan Avenue, Chicago, IL 60601.

Write and Sell Your TV Drama by Ann Loring & Evelyn Kaye. Writing to sell. 87 pp. $21.80 ppd. ALEK Publishing, 223 Tenafly Road, Englewood, NJ 07631.

T.V. Scriptwriter's Handbook by Alfred Brenner. What to write, how to write and the marketplace. 324 pp. $11.45 ppd. Writer's Digest Books, 9933 Alliance Road, Bldg P, Cincinnati, OH 45242.

The Complete Book of Scriptwriting by J. Michael Straczynski. Radio, television, stage, motion pictures. Art, craft and marketing. 269 pp. $16.45 ppd. Writer's Digest Books, 9933 Alliance Road, Bldg P, Cincinnati, OH 45242.

Writing for the Soaps by Jean Rouverol. How to write for television soap operas. Examples. Resources. 219 pp. $16.45 ppd. Writer's Digest Books, 9933 Alliance Road, Bldg P, Cincinnati, OH 45242.

Scriptwriters Market. Advice and directory. 100 pp. $22.95 ppd. Joshua Publishing, 8033 Sunset Blvd #306, Hollywood, CA 90046.

How to Write a Play by Raymond Hull. Stage play writing formula. 240 pp. $15.45 ppd. Writer's Digest Books, 9933 Alliance Road, Bldg P, Cincinnati, OH 45242.

Periodicals

Hollywood Scriptletter. Advice on agents and markets. 1626 North Wilcox #385, Hollywood, CA 90028.

RELIGIOUS BOOKS

Write for the Religion Market by John A. Moore. Directed mainly toward writing newspaper and magazine articles. 128 pp. Hardcover. $9.95 ppd. ETC Publications, P.O. Dwr. 1627- A, Palm Springs, CA 92263.

DIRECTORIES

How to Publish a Directory of Home Based Businesses for Fun and Profit by Don Vandeventer and Paula Vineyard. 54 pp. H.B.D. Publications, 4711 Ottawa Road, Rockford, IL 61107.

MANUALS

Publishing a Manual. How to write, edit, typeset, layout, print and bind a sport certification manual. 67 pp. $3.50. Coaching Association of Canada. 333 River Road, Ottawa, Ontario K1L 8H9, Canada.

COMBINATIONS

The Writer's Manual. Covers the mechanics, fiction, nonfiction, and has sections on children, poetry, scripts, and dissertations. Section on composition. 987 pp. $21.95 ppd. ETC Publications, P.O. Dwr ETC, Palm Springs, CA 92263-1608.

PUBLISHING

The Self-Publishing Manual, How to Write, Print & Sell Your Own Book by Dan Poynter. The faster, surer, more profitable way to becoming a published author. A manual on book promotion. 352 pp. $14.95 Para Publishing, P.O. Box 4232-P, Santa Barbara, CA 93140-4232.

The Writer Publisher by Charles N. Aronson. Entertaining yet sobering coverage of the author's problems with a vanity publisher and his discovery and mastering of self-publishing. Good reading. If you are even considering vanity publishing, you must read this book. 369 pp. $4.95 Charles N. Aronson, RR#1, Hundred Acres, Arcade, NY 14009.

How to Get Happily Published by Judith Appelbaum & Nancy Evans. How to approach a publisher. Best (most realistic) view of publishing from New York. Resources. 271 pp. $7.95 New American Library/Plume.

The Writer's Survival Manual by Carol Meyer. Good view of trade publishing by a managing editor at HBJ. Packed with information. 310 pp. $4.95. Bantam.

Getting Published: The Educator's Resource Book by Joel Levin. How and where to get published in the educational market with a list of magazine and book publishers. 281 pp. $12.95 ppd. Arco Publishing, Inc., 215 Park Avenue South, New York, NY 10003.

Into Print, *A Practical Guide to Writing, Illustrating and Publishing* by Mary Hill and Wendell Cochran. Heaviest on the mechanics of production. 178 pp. $6.95. William Kaufmann, Inc. One First Street, Los Altos, CA 94022.

How to Understand & Negotiate a Book Contract or Magazine Agreement by Richard Balkin. Negotiating and contracting. 156 pp. $13.45 ppd. Writer's Digest Books, 9933 Alliance Road, Bldg P, Cincinnati, OH 45242.

LEGAL ADVICE

Author Law & Strategies by Brad Bunnin and Peter Beren. Contracts, collaboration, agents, defamation, right of privacy, copyright, etc. Examples and resources. 294 pp. $14.95 Nolo Press, 950 Parker Street, Berkeley, CA 94710.

RESOURCES

Office Purchasing Guide: *How to Save up to 50% on Office Supplies, Furniture, etc.* by Tod Snodgrass. Money saving tips. 254 pp. $17.95 Lowen Publishing, P.O. Box 6870-P, Torrance, CA 90504-0870.

Freelancers of North America 1984-1985 Marketplace. Lists editors, copywriters, speechwriters, ghostwriters, collaborators, business, technical and medical writers. 301 pp. $32.95 Author Aid/Research Associates International, 340 East 52nd Street, New York, NY 10022.

Literary Agents of North America Marketplace. Lists agents and collaboration/ghostwriting services. 135 pp. $16.95 Author Aid/Research Associates International, 340 East 52nd Street, New York, NY 10022.

International Directory of Little Magazines and Small Presses by Len Fulton and Ellen Ferber. Complete information on over 3,500 book publishers and magazines. 645 pp. $18.95 Dustbooks, P.O. Box 100-P, Paradise, CA 95969.

COMPUTERS/WORD PROCESSORS

Word Processors & Information Processing, *A Basic Manual on What They Are and How to Buy* by Dan Poynter. Using a computer to write articles and books. Explains functions and features. Resources. 170 pp. $11.95 Para Publishing, P.O. Box 4232-P, Santa Barbara, CA 93140-4232.

Computer Selection Guide, *Choosing the Right Hardware and Software: Business-Professional-Personal* by Dan Poynter. Explanations, comparitive charts, resources. 164 pp. $11.95 Para Publishing, P.O. Box 4232-P, Santa Barbara, CA 93140-4232.

BROCHURES ON BOOKS of interest to writers and publishers are available from:

R.R. Bowker Catalog
P.O. Box 1807
Ann Arbor, MI 48106

Direct Marketing Assn.
6 East 54rd Street
New York, NY 10017

Dustbooks,
P.O. Box 100-P
Paradise, CA 95969

Gale Research Co.
Book Tower
Detroit, MI 48226

Knowledge Industry Publications
701 Westchester Avenue
White Plains, NY 10604

Para Publishing
P.O. Box 4232-P
Santa Barbara, CA 93140- 4232

Ross Book Service
P.O. Box 12093-P
Seminary, Alexandria, VA 22304

Self-Publishing Book Review
Ad-Lib Publications
John Kremer
P.O. Box 1102-P
Fairfield, IA 52556

Self-Publishers Book Store
P.O. Box 2038-P
Vancouver, WA 98661

J. Whitaker & Sons Ltd.
12 Dyott Street
London WC1A 1DF
Great Britain

The Writer, Inc.
120-P Boylston Street
Boston, MA 02116

Writer's Digest Books
9933-P Alliance Road, Bldg P
Cincinnati, OH 45242

REFERENCE BOOKS AND DIRECTORIES may be used and previewed at the reference desk in your local library. Write to the publishers for ordering details.

From: R.R. Bowker Company, P. O. Box 1807, Ann Arbor, MI 48106.

Literary Market Place. Very important. Lists agents, artists, associations, book clubs, reviewers, exporters, magazines, newspapers, news services, radio & T.V., and many other services. Annual.

International Literary Market Place. Lists publishers, agents, suppliers, etc. in 160 countries outside the U.S. and Canada.

Books in Print. List all books currently available by subject, title and author. Annual.

> *Paperbound Books in Print.* Lists all softcover books currently available by subject, title and author as well as addresses of publishers.

> *Subject Guide to Forthcoming Books.* A preview. Bimonthly. Nonfiction.

From: Dustbooks, P. O. Box 100-P, Paradise, CA 95969.

International Directory of Magazines and Small Presses.
Small Press Record of Books in Print.
Directory of Small Magazines/Press Editors and Publishers.
Directory of Poetry Publishers

From: Writer's Digest, 9933 Alliance Road, Cincinnati, OH 45242.

Writer's Market. Lists over 5,000 paying markets for writing, etc.

Writer's Yearbook. Information on writing, markets, etc. *Writer's Digest* also publishes market directories for photographers, artists, song writers and craft workers.

MAGAZINES FOR AUTHORS
Write for a sample copy and current subscription rates.

ALA Booklist (book reviews)
American Library Association
50 East Huron Street
Chicago, IL 60611

American Bookseller (bookstore news)
122 East 42nd Street
New York, NY 10017

Canadian Author & Bookman
P.O. Box 120
Niagara-On-The-Lake, ON
Canada LOS IJO

Library Journal
R.R. Bowker Co.
P.O. Box 67
Whitinsville, MA 01588

Publishers Weekly
R.R. Bowker Co.
P.O. Box 67
Whitinsville, MA 01588
This is the magazine of the publishing industry.

Small Press Magazine
205 East 42nd Street
New York, NY 10036

Small Press Review
P.O. Box 100-P
Paradise, CA 95969
Len Fulton's magazine for authors and publishers.

West Coast Review of Books
1501 North Hobart Blvd.
Hollywood, CA 90027

The Writer
120-P Boylston Street
Boston, MA 02116

Writer's Digest
9933 Alliance Road, Bldg P
Cincinnati, OH 45242
Inspiring and useful reading for writers.

NEWSLETTERS FOR AUTHORS
Write for a sample copy and current subscription rates.

Author's Newsletter
P.O. Box 32008-P
Phoenix, AZ 85064

Inkling
P.O. Box 128-P
Alexandria, MN 56308

Editorial Eye
5905-P Pratt Street
Alexandria, VA 22310

Towers Club USA Newsletter
Jerry Buchanan
P.O. Box 2038-P
Vancouver, WA 98668

Information Marketing Letter
Mark Nolan
P.O. Box 2234
Eugene, OR 97402

Writer's Connection
10601 South de Anza Blvd., #301
Cupertino, CA 95014

PAMPHLETS AND REPORTS OF INTEREST TO AUTHORS AND PUBLISHERS. Write for latest prices.

Dustbooks
P.O. Box 100-P
Paradise, CA 95969
1. *Book Publishing Agreement* by Richard Balkin. 60¢

Federal Trade Commission
Washington, DC 20580
1. *Consumer Alert - The Vanity Press News* release dated 19 July 1959
2. *Vanity Press Findings.* Dockets 7005 and 7489.

P. E. N. American Center
47 Fifth Avenue
New York, NY 10003
1. *Grants and Awards Available to American Writers.* $2.25

McHugh Publishing Reports
92 Hartford Street
Framingham, MA 01701
1. *Permissions, Copyright and Fair Use: A Guide for Book Publishing Managers.*

Literature Program
National Endowment for the Arts
2401 E Street NW
Washington, DC 20506
1. Assistance, fellowships and residencies for writers.

Poets & Writers, Inc.
201 West 54th Street
New York, NY 10019
1. *Awards List.* $2.50
2. *The Sponsors List.* $2.50
3. *Literary Bookstores in the U.S.*
4. *Writers Guide to Copyright.*
5. *Dir. American Poets and Fiction Writers.* $16.95

The Copyright Office
Office of Public Affairs
Library of Congress
Washington, DC 20559
1. *General Guide to the Copyright Act of 1976*

Writer's Digest Books
9933-P Alliance Road
Cincinnati, OH 45242
1. *Getting Started in Writing*
2. *Jobs & Opportunities For Writers*
3. *Does it Pay to Pay to Have it Published?*

PROFESSIONAL ORGANIZATIONS
Write for an application and inquire about benefits and dues. Many associations publish a magazine or newsletters. For a more complete list of writer's associations, see Writer's Market and the *International Directory of Writers' Groups & Associations* (The Inkling, P.O. Box 128, Alexandria, MN 56308. $19.50).

American Medical Writers
Association
5272 River Road #290
Bethesda, MD 20016

The Authors Guild
234 West 44th Street
New York, NY 10036

Aviation/Space Writers Association
1000 Connecticut Avenue NW
#707
Washington, DC 20006

Mystery Writers of America
105 East 19th Street
New York, NY 10003

National Association of Science
Writers
P.O. Box 294
Greenlawn, NY 11740

The National Writers Club
1450 South Havana #620-P
Aurora, CO 80012

Poets & Writers, Inc.
201 West 54th Street
New York, NY 10019

Science Fiction Writers of America
68 Countryside Apts
Hackettstown, NJ 07840

Society of American Travel Writers
1120 Connecticut Avenue NW #940
Washington, DC 20036

Western Writers of America
Rt #1, Box 35H
Victor, MT 59875

INDEX

COLOPHON

This book was completely produced with computerized equipment. The authors used computers for gathering and filing information as well as for writing, editing and even setting the type. This book is an example of typesetting with a computer.

PRODUCTION NOTES

Composition
    Input:
        IBM Personal Computer XT
        Xerox model 860 word processor
    Output:
        Conversion to IBM Displaywriter by
        Text Sciences Corporation, Santa Monica, CA

        Typesetting codes keyed on to manuscript disks

        Type generated from coded disks by
        Graphic Typesetting Service, L.A., CA
    Typestyles:
        Text, Palatino
        Headlines, Helvetica
        Quotes, Souvenir
    Book Design-Production:
        One-to-One Book Production, Glendale, CA
    Cover art:
        Robert Howard

Paper:
    Text, 60-pound white offset book
    Cover, 12 pt. C1S white

Ink:
    Text, standard black
    Cover, four colors with film lamination

Printing:
    Offset lithography, McNaughton & Gunn
    Ann Arbor, Michigan

Binding:
    Perfect (adhesive)

Edition:
    First edition: 10,000

IS THERE AN AUTHOR IN YOUR LIFE?

I know the following people have a book inside them and I want to help. Please send them a FREE writing/publishing information kit.

Name:_____

Address:_____

City:_____State: _____Zip:_____

Name:_____

Address:_____

City:____ _____State: _____Zip:____

Name:_____

Address:_____

City:_____State: _____Zip:_____

Name:_____

Address:_____

City:_____State: _____Zip:_____

Mail this form to Para Publishing, P. O. Box 4232-P, Santa Barbara, CA 93140-4232

ORDER FORM

Para Publishing
Post Office 4232-P
Santa Barbara, CA 93140-4232, USA
Telephone (805) 968-7277

Please send me the following books:

See the book descriptions in the Appendix.

The following books are must reading if you plan to author a book. Check your library and favorite bookstore or order from **Para Publishing.**

QUANTITY		AMOUNT
_____	The Self-Publishing Manual, $14.95 by Dan Poynter	_____
_____	Author Law & Strategies, $14.95 by Drad Bunnin and Peter Beren	_____
_____	How to Get Happily Published, $7.95 by Judith Appelbaum & Nancy Evans	_____
_____	Write Right!, $4.95 by Jan Venolia	_____

Other books by Dan Poynter

_____	Is There A Book Inside You?, $9.95	_____
_____	Computer Selection Guide, $11.95	_____
_____	Word Processors, $11.95	_____
_____	Publishing Short-Run Books, $5.95	_____
_____	Business Letters for Publishers, $14.95	_____
_____	Book Fairs, $7.95	_____
_____	Publishing Forms, $14.95	_____

— continued on next page

Also use this form for ordering Mindy Bingham's bestselling books for young people.

QUANTITY   **AMOUNT**

_____   Choices, A Teen Woman's Journal for
            Self-awareness and Personal Planning, $12.95   _____

_____   Challenges, A Young Man's Journal for
            Self-awareness and Personal Planning $12.95   _____

Total for books _____

Shipping: $1.00 first book _____
50¢ each additional book

California residents please add 6% sales tax _____

AMOUNT ENCLOSED (U.S. funds) _____

I understand that I may return any book for a full-refund if not satisfied.

Name:_____

Address:_____

City:_____State:_____Zip:_____

☐ I can't wait 3-4 weeks for Book Rate. Here is $3.00 per book for Air Mail.

☐ Please add my name to the *Book Inside Grapevine* so that I may receive more information on writing and publishing.

☐ Please send me information on Dan Poynter's publishing weekend workshops in Santa Barbara, California.

ORDER FORM

Para Publishing
Post Office 4232-P
Santa Barbara, CA 93140-4232, USA
Telephone (805) 968-7277

Please send me the following books:

See the book descriptions in the Appendix.

The following books are must reading if you plan to author a book. Check your library and favorite bookstore or order from **Para Publishing.**

QUANTITY		AMOUNT
_____	The Self-Publishing Manual, $14.95 by Dan Poynter	_____
_____	Author Law & Strategies, $14.95 by Brad Bunnin and Peter Beren	_____
_____	How to Get Happily Published, $7.95 by Judith Appelbaum & Nancy Evans	_____
_____	Write Right!, $4.95 by Jan Venolia	_____

Other books by Dan Poynter

_____	Is There A Book Inside You?, $9.95	_____
_____	Computer Selection Guide, $11.95	_____
_____	Word Processors, $11.95	_____
_____	Publishing Short-Run Books, $5.95	_____
_____	Business Letters for Publishers, $14.95	_____
_____	Book Fairs, $7.95	_____
_____	Publishing Forms, $14.95	_____

— **continued on next page**

Also use this form for ordering Mindy Bingham's bestselling books for young people.

QUANTITY   **AMOUNT**

_____   Choices, A Teen Woman's Journal for
Self-awareness and Personal Planning, $12.95   _____

_____   Challenges, A Young Man's Journal for
Self-awareness and Personal Planning $12.95   _____

Total for books _____

Shipping: $1.00 first book _____
50¢ each additional book

California residents please add 6% sales tax _____

AMOUNT ENCLOSED (U.S. funds) _____

I understand that I may return any book for a full-refund if not satisfied.

Name:_____

Address:_____

City:_____State:_____Zip:_____

☐ I can't wait 3-4 weeks for Book Rate. Here is $3.00 per book for Air Mail.

☐ Please add my name to the *Book Inside Grapevine* so that I may receive more information on writing and publishing.

☐ Please send me information on Dan Poynter's publishing weekend workshops in Santa Barbara, California.